From **SHACKLES**
(Badge #741)

to *Freedom*
(Inmate #429-490)

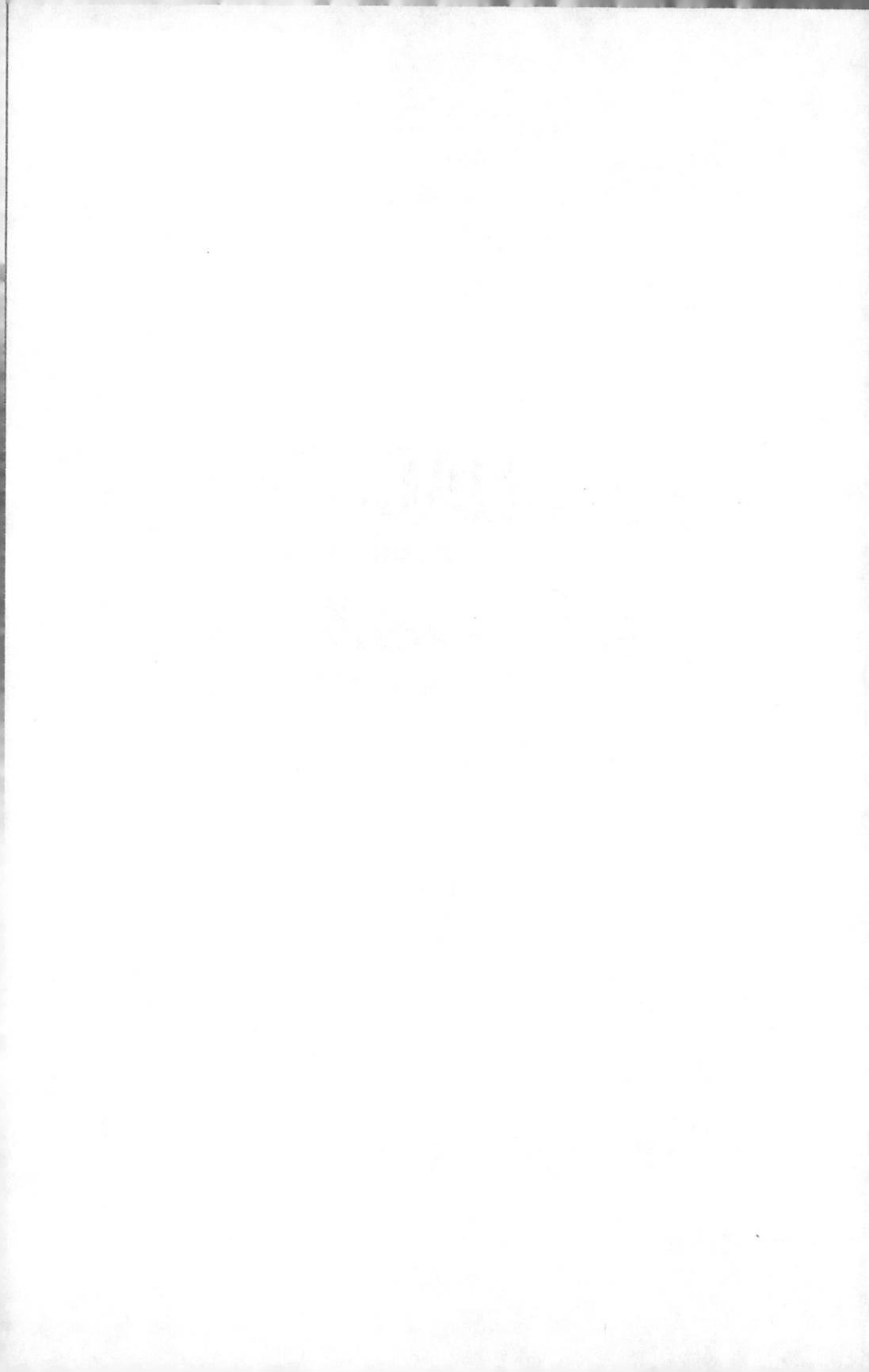

From **SHACKLES**
(Badge #741)
to *Freedom*
(Inmate #429-490)

LUKE MCCORMICK

PTP

Pure Thoughts Publishing, LLC

www.PureThoughtsPublishing.com

Conyers, GA

CONTENTS

ACKNOWLEDGMENTS

I am grateful to the following people for their love and perseverance through this trying time:

My loving wife, Kathy: Thank you for inspiring me and encouraging me to complete this process. You are an amazing woman….my gift from God. You are my anchor.

My Mother: I've heard it said, there's no bond like that of a mother and a son. You not only taught me that, but you proved it every single day for 10 years. Thank you mom, for being my mom.

Tiffy, Lolo and LT: I was taken from your lives at such young ages, yet, I was never taken from your hearts. Thank you for showing me that my physical absence never took away the "Daddy" in your hearts.

My Family: Thank you for your undying, unwavering, love, care, and support of me over the many years of turmoil. Because of you, I now know the "true" meaning of the word "family." I love you all!

In loving memory to those that I lost: Daddy, and Grandma Bertha and Rosie: Though I missed your home going, your memories are alive in me. I miss you.

DEDICATION

For "Him"

To God be the glory. For He is my strength and my firm foundation. In Him I live, move and have my being.

INTRODUCTION

I was an Ohio Highway Patrol State Trooper for nine and a half years. For two of those years, I was a plain clothes Investigator. During my career, I had received numerous awards and specialized training. In 1993, I received a letter of commendation from the Governor of the state, and in 1994 was selected State Trooper of the year by my peers at the patrol post to which I was assigned. In 1995, I received the Police Officers of the year award which is given to an officer which stood amongst others from other agencies and departments, and I also received the Mothers against Drunk Driving (M.A.D.D.) award twice consecutively. I received training with the Secret Service, Coroners Investigations, provided protection for dignitaries such as the President of the United States, the Secretary of State, Governors and other such dignitaries. I enforced the law, yet treated all that I came across with utmost respect. I absolutely loved my job, and I served the state of Ohio with pride, integrity and honor. Yet, all the years of service – all the awards, accolades, recognition and honor, was all stripped from me in one nights time. None of the training I ever received could have possibly prepared me for the events of one night. A night that forever changed the course of my life.

THE COURTROOM

Here I was a nine and a half year veteran with the State Highway Patrol. A State Trooper with no blot or blemish on my career or record. But one night, I did something that I've done a thousand times- something you hear about but think it can never happen to you. Something that changed my life *forever*. While unloading my service weapon, a round discharged and struck my wife. And even though deep within the both of us, we knew otherwise, we confessed it as being an accidental discharge. I was placed on administrative leave, though no charges were filed against me. Within a few weeks' time, I was terminated. I felt abandoned and ostracized by people whom I considered friends on the State Patrol for many years. Everyone was told not to have any contact or communication with me. For the first time, while being a State Trooper, I felt alone.

A year went by and as I was left trying to pick up the pieces of my life. I found myself sitting in a court room being indicted on the charge of felonious assault against my wife. What's so astonishing to me is the fact that from day one, my wife told the prosecutors, detectives, and even the Grand Jury that this was an accident.

The week and a half of the jury trial was, at *that* time, the worst thing I'd ever gone through or experienced. I had to sit there day after day, and listen to my name, my character and my life being tarnished. I had lost my job doing something I loved, and this happened before I was ever charged for a single crime. And now, I was looking at losing something even more precious, my freedom.

Each day after the trial, which lasted for several days, I would go home and be surrounded by family and friends who filled me with love and support, but nothing could comfort me. I was like a walking zombie, who was truly on the verge of a breakdown. I was so out of touch with everything around me, and out of touch with reality itself. It was as if I knew nothing all at once, at a single moment in time. This was the most elongated year of my entire life.

The trial ended, and the jury began its deliberation. My mind was going in all sorts of directions. I remember one evening, after waiting for a decision, while mowing the lawn, I heard a voice from deep within me say, *"This is the last time you'll ever cut this grass."* I pushed that lawnmower and cried like a baby. *Oh!* I could feel my life spiraling to depths of unmitigated despair. All attempts to console me were futile, no matter what I did, or how much others tried. My smile was gone, and there was no bringing it back. My laugh, my joy, all the simple things had vanished. I couldn't enjoy my kids like I used to, and that made me feel worse than anything else. All of me, inside and out, seemed to be dying, and I knew it. I felt it.

The next day was the third day of jury deliberations, and I was standing outside the courthouse with my brother-in-law and a couple of friends. Suddenly, a short black man walked past me, glaring deeply into my eyes. As he passed, he said to me, *"I don't know who you are brother, but you're going to be alright."* I looked at him; his eyes pierced my soul with a warmth and calmness. Unable to take my eyes off of him, I watched as he turned back toward the courthouse entrance, his eyes too, never leaving me. I stood in astonishment, and pondered what he had just said. He returned and sat near me on some steps just away from the building. I wanted to thank him for the encouraging and much needed words that he had spoken to me, so I approached him not knowing exactly what to say other than *"thank you!"* I leaned over his left shoulder, and before I could say a word, he looked straight ahead and said, *"I'm not going to tell you anymore, it's already done, praise Me ahead of time."* His words literally staggered me, and I was in shock! I quickly went over to the people that were standing outside with me, but nobody else saw him.

I went back into the courthouse, and I had the most overwhelming feeling that I had just spoken with an angel of God. I could feel myself shaking as I raced to one of my sisters to tell her what I just experienced. Just then, another man came running down the hall from another courtroom *screaming, "God is still on the throne!"* He yelled this until he disappeared into the elevator! When he did, a woman stepped out and began to quietly sing a verse of a song in the most beautiful tone. *"No weapon formed against me shall prosper."* I instantly recognized this as a verse of scripture that my mother and niece stood on throughout the trial. I began pacing in circles in the hallway, raising my hands in the air and praising God. At that moment, I was so caught up spiritually, giving the Lord all the glory, for I *thought,* my trial of affliction was over. Little did I know it was just about to begin.

My family and friends stood in the hallway outside the courtroom, and a very *still, soft* bell rang. My attorney came out of the courtroom and advised me that the jury had reached a verdict. I watched as my family entered the courtroom filled with terror and hope. The media rustled in also. I stayed back, hugged my wife, and placed the keys to my car in her hands, and she also reluctantly entered the courtroom. My attorney and I then stood alone, and as we shook hands and embraced, he whispered, *"No matter the outcome Luke, it's been a pleasure working with you."* With those words, we entered the courtroom together. I entered, the media had their cameras plastered in my face and dead silence smothered the room. The jury entered, and I felt my entire being sitting in the pit of my stomach. Then one word broke through the silence of the room like a thief in the night. *"Guilty!"* My spirit, my heart, my soul – left me. Instantly, I heard crying, though I didn't know who it was. I remember looking back at one of my sisters and seeing her face filled with shock. The deputies placed handcuffs on me and quickly escorted me out of the courtroom. I could not bear to look back at my wife or my mother, but I did, and my heart was crushed.

COUNTY JAIL

When I arrived at the Montgomery County Jail, I was devastated! I felt as though all hope was gone. All I could remember was my wife and mother crying on my sister's shoulder.

The deputy then began to process me, and I was told to strip so they could search me for contraband, and I felt a strong sense of being degraded. Stark reality hit me as I was taken out of my nice suit, and placed in blue jail clothing. I felt so belittled and shameful, and more naked than I already was. The deputies took my wallet and emptied the contents. Tears whelped within my eyes when I saw pictures of my children. I couldn't help but wonder when I would see them again, or touch them once more. I was placed in a cold, empty cell with a concrete bench style seat that was cold and hard to the touch. A toilet with no seat sat where you had no sense of privacy. I dropped my head in my lap, and sobbed heavily. I cried out to God and asked Him,

"Why? I just don't understand God! Why did you let this happen? Why did you just send me an angel, telling me it was done and to praise you ahead of time? God, why did you let this happen?" I sat on that cold concrete bench and began to pound my fist in anger. I again screamed out, *"I don't understand God! I don't understand! Please help me Jesus!"* I looked up and noticed another jail inmate working inside the lobby area of the jail where others wait to be processed. I saw him as he looked up at the television, and obviously there I was once again on the news. He looked in at me, and shook his head as if to say, *"I'm sorry for you man."* For a few seconds, I was given a little burst of empathy in my soul from this man, and he had no idea how much I needed that. I again began

to cry out to God, but God was silent. I heard – I felt – nothing. All I could think about was my wife, wondering how she was doing, and that made me cry all the more. The fear of not knowing took on a whole new meaning for me. A deputy then came to my cell, *"Mr. McCormick, come with me."* I was moved to another cell because they had kids coming in for a field trip. I thought, *"Great.* Not only is my face all over the news, but now I'm going to be on display." But the deputies treated me fair, very well actually, and didn't let them see me. I was placed in a cell smaller than the first one and even colder. It seemed the more I continued to cry, the quieter God was. I looked out in the lobby, and it was full of people waiting to be processed. I knew I was all over the news, and I know other criminals hate law enforcement, which in their eyes, I was one of them. Fortunately, another deputy came to my cell, and I was finally able to contact my family. I attempted to call my wife, but she was not home. I stood there crying, saying *"God please let me get a hold of someone."* I knew I couldn't bear to call my mother, so I called my baby sister, and my brother-in-law answered. I was a complete mess as he told me to try and be strong, and no matter what, he was with me. Then my sister got on the phone, and that did it. Tears flowed, and all I could muster to say to her was, *"I don't know what to do!"* Since our childhood, I can never remember seeing or hearing her cry until that moment. I never want to hear that sound again. All I could hear in the background was her crying her heart out, so much so that my brother-in-law had to come back to the phone because she wasn't able. I couldn't take it, and felt as though I was going to pass out from sorrow. I just asked him to please get a hold of my wife for me, which he promised he would. I've never felt so alone and devastated in my life. I literally did not know what to do!

Two deputies took me to what they called a *Pod* and told me I would be separated from the general population. One deputy looked at me and said, *"Man I know this is hard for you, but we are going to make you as comfortable as possible under the circumstances."* While on the elevator, the other deputy said, *"If you have any problems, or you need anything, just let someone know."* It was then; I began to feel the favor of God.

I was placed in a cell about the size of my bathroom at home. It had two bunk beds, a small table with a chair and a toilet. I collapsed in the chair, placed my face in hands, and sobbed really hard uncontrollably. I again said, *"God please – please help me. I need you Lord, please. I don't know what to do."* Once more, God was silent.

About an hour later, a deputy opened my cell door and informed me that I had an attorney visit. I was escorted to a room where sat my attorney's father who runs the firm. We talked briefly, my mind and heart felt so hollow, as again I cried with each word I tried to speak. All I can remember him saying was *"This is going to be the longest night of your life."* What he didn't realize, was that it already was. I asked why he had come instead of his son. He replied that his son was to hurt to see me and felt to blame for the outcome.

I was then escorted back to my cell, and the deputy asked me if I needed anything. The one thing I needed, he couldn't provide, so I softly said *"No sir."* I began to realize that even in the midst of my worst of times, God *still* has grace, for He allowed me to have favor with the deputies, and I was able to struggle within silently to thank Him for it.

A little later my cell door again was opened and another deputy asked if I wanted to come out for a while, for during this time all the other jail inmates were locked in their cells. I walked out into this pod, and I could feel so many eyes watching me. It was as though I was walking through some type of time zone, and I was the only living person around; though I knew there was someone else out there. I attempted to call my wife, but was unable to reach her, so I decided to call my mother. *"Oh!"* What a mistake that was. My Mom was in worse shape than I was. I could tell she was trying to sound strong for me, but I know my mother, and I believe that hurt me even more. My mother and I are a lot alike and I know she was as devastated as I was! I am my mother's only son out of five children, and there is no bond like that of a son and his mother. Together, and by the grace of God, we were able to make it through the conversation, though the pain never subsided. She told me to be strong, and to know that God was going to work this all out. My mother always had a way to make things better, even when she was hurting so deeply.

I asked the deputy how much longer I could stay out, to which he replied, *"Take your time Mr. McCormick."* I again tried my wife, and this time I heard this voice say *"Hello."* I completely lost it then – tears, slobber, everything I had left in me poured out at that moment. I remember looking up at the other cell doors and seeing other inmates looking at me, but I didn't care. All I could focus on was that voice on the other end of the phone, that voice that I knew I had hurt. At that time, I was talking to the one voice I wanted to hear other than God's. She told me to be strong and to keep my faith and trust in the Lord. But something was strange about her, something I could feel and hear in her voice, yet couldn't grasp the understanding. She wasn't crying, wasn't distraught, and actually had a sense of easiness about her. For me, almost too easy.

I went back to my cell, tears again filled my eyes. Actually, they never left me. Again I prayed and asked God why this happened to me. Why did the verdict come back *guilty?* Especially when He sent His angel to tell me *"It's already done, praise me ahead of time."* I pleaded for Him to *please* talk to me, and to tell me why this happened. Though in the core of my soul I knew, and I knew God did to. I knew why He was so silent to me.

The afternoon passed. I heard them bringing food trays in for the dinner meal. I heard a light knock on my cell door, and when I looked up, I saw a friend of mine that I grew up with standing there. He looked at me with what seemed to be tears in his eyes and silently motioned for me to keep my head up. It took all I had to muster within me to simply wave and nod my head as if to say *"thank you!"* I later learned he was a supervisor with the food service department at the jail. When I saw him, it gave me mixed emotions. Part of me was happy to see a friendly face, someone I knew, though in part I was largely embarrassed and ashamed for him to see me this way. He had the deputy open my door and as he approached me we embraced, and he discreetly handed me an ice cold soda. With tears whelping in my eyes I reflected back to when I used to play basketball with him and his brothers, and was left to wonder if I'd ever see those days again. Now he's free to do as he pleased, while I'm imprisoned, not able to even get a glimpse of the outside.

I was stuck in the reflection of my thoughts and really getting down on myself when my cell door suddenly was opened and another inmate was bringing me my food tray. I thanked him, and he said, *"God bless you brother."* I watched with rigorous pain in my heart as he walked away and my cell door closed. Tears dropped into my tray while praying over my food as I felt God quietly, softly, tugging at my heart. At the time, I couldn't comprehend this nudging within me, though I was soon to discover.

After dinner was over, I was told that I could come out for what's called recreation time. I learned that this is when inmates are out of their cells to socialize, watch television, play cards, etc. Though being separated from the general population, I noticed a few guys out of their cells as well, who I later discovered were trustees who had special privileges for cleaning the jail. I noticed the same inmate who earlier brought my tray to my cell sitting at a table by himself. Famished for human contact, I approached and asked if he minded if I sat with him. He said to me *"please do my brother."* This man had a very calm demeanor as he shared with me why he was locked up. He told me how he was caught up with drugs, but how God had since turned his life around. Tears came to my eyes as I began to share with him my situation, when he abruptly stopped me. *"I know who you are, and I'm not here to judge you. I love you as a brother in Christ."* He went on to tell me that he had been praying for me, and that God told him to tell me that *He* has me here to *"Focus on Him and His word."* He spoke, and I felt a sudden calmness within my spirit. He and I talked for a little while longer and he asked if I had a Bible with me to which I said I didn't. After the conversation I called my wife and mother to tell them about my encounter with this man. I wanted to give them some glimmer of hope as well. My mother told me, *"Well Luke, you know what you have to do."* She said she knew God had something for me to do and that He had to separate me from my wife so I could perform His will. At the time, I didn't understand that statement, but I did begin to understand now why I had the tugging within my heart. She told me to be strong and praise God no matter what. Just continue to give Him praise. Her words took me back to the man in the front of the courthouse. *"Praise*

Me ahead of time." I love my mother so much. She is such a source of inspiration for me.

I went back to my cell. The inmate I talked with handed me a Bible. He explained that he had an extra one. He said, *"I know you're looking for a miracle, but the miracle is you."* I fell to my knees, raised my hands and cried out, *"I surrender all. Mind, heart, soul body and spirit – I surrender all!"* My tears of pain and sorrow turned to tears of praise and worship. All that night and the next day, I prayed and praised and worshiped. God began to speak to me through His word, as I read a verse of scripture in the book of Isaiah 55:8-9:

> *For my thoughts are not your thoughts, neither are your ways My ways. For as the Heavens are higher than the earth, so are My ways higher than your ways, and my thoughts than your thoughts.*

The feeling of being in jail for me personifies description. I felt like my faith was on trial, just as I was only hours ago. I began right then to learn not to question my circumstance, only to trust Him.

———◆◆◆———

I woke from my first night in jail, and felt like a kid lost in a rain storm. *My God!* I've never had as much as a speeding ticket, now here I am in a blue suit labeled *Montgomery County Jail Inmate.* I'm now known to society as a convicted felon. Yet, God says *"Trust Me!"* This is a level of trust I've never before experienced, and as I looked around the cell at the walls, the floor, the sink and toilet, this same trust was beginning to waver. For all I truly wanted was to be home with my family. It was then a knock came at my cell door; a knock that was the beginning of change in my life.

An inmate slid a note under my door, smiled, and waved briskly, and walked away before the officers could see him. In this note, he introduced himself, told me he was a Christian brother, and that he had prayed for me. He told me that Jesus had a calling on my life and

He wanted me to form a *personal* relationship with Him, by reading His Word. Suddenly and unexpectedly, this man, through this note, wrote the story of my life. It was as though he's been walking within the conscience of my soul. I looked out my cell door to get a glimpse of this man so I could thank him, at which time he pointed to another cell across the pod from mine. I noticed a middle aged man waving and smiling at me, and I realized he was the one who wrote this note and had the trustee slide it under my door. I smiled and waved back to this man, and though I had no idea who he was, I felt a sort of calming presence radiating from across the pod. I began to pace the cell and think of God's confirmation and what was beginning to happen with me. Just then my cell door popped open and the officer standing there told me I had a visit. I instantly got overjoyed and wiped my tears because I was finally going to see my family since the verdict came out. While being escorted, the officer asked me how I was holding up. I told him I was doing the best I could under the circumstance, though I felt my inner man crumbling in decay. I was again nourished with words of comfort as he told me I'd get through this. I only wished I too could believe that.

We arrived at the visiting room and I saw my wife, mother and two of my sisters sitting there behind the glass partition. They had smiles on their faces when they saw me which lit my heart aglow. The officer told me that visits are usually thirty minute sessions, but winked, and he said for me to stay until he came to get me. He smiled, as I whispered *"Thank you; I appreciate that,"* to which he responded, *"No problem."* Though now in a blue outfit, I felt through him a sense of respect to a fallen comrade. The entire department gave me this feeling, and I not only appreciated it – I needed it.

I spoke to my family through the phone on the wall, and whether it was being done on my behalf or not, they couldn't wipe the smiles from their faces. They all took turns talking with me, telling me that I looked good. I believe that they were afraid of how I would look, because of the emotional state I was in during the time of the trial. The look in their eyes was as though I'd gone through a total transformation overnight. *Oh!* I'd never been so happy to see someone in all my life! I couldn't take my gaze off of them. *God!* I missed them so badly, and I had only been one day removed from them. I was stricken with so much grief when I looked into my wife's eyes, and all I wanted to do was to grasp her by her shoulders and tell her *"I'm sorry."* But I couldn't, and that was a weighty strain.

I asked about my children, and they assured me they were fine. The anguish of thinking of them was so overwhelming, and I began to grieve profoundly, as tears trickled down my face. My sister seeing this, told me to remember all that God had said, and that His word cannot lie. I knew they were doing all they could to uplift me, though I wasn't doing my part for them. We were allowed to visit for almost an hour before the deputy came to get me. With tears in my eyes, I told them I loved them, blew them a kiss, and they seemed to vanish like a dream of the night. Walking back to my cell, I thanked the officer, and was left to reminisce about vivid memories, of times gone by.

———◆———

Days and nights flashed by like a shimmer of light, yet at the same time lingered forever. I called my wife and mother every day, leaning on them for comfort and support. I knew I had to one day make a phone call that would be extremely strenuous to my heart. Though I knew it was one where I'd have to show myself to be strong, still, the thought of making it made me fearful. I had to call my children.

I placed the call, and my oldest daughter answered; Oh! Her voice was so wholesome. I dug deep within, knowing she was feeding off me and hanging onto my every word. Even though my heart was aching, I had to endure this for her. I told her how much I loved her and needed her to be strong for her younger sister and brother for me. Though he doesn't like talking on the phone, my son, my little man – spoke with me. We were talking about his football practices, which just days before I was on the sidelines watching. He then asked me a question that melted – crushed – my heart. He asked, *"Daddy, will you be able to come to my next practice?"* I choked back tears as it took every ounce of whatever was left in me to not let my boy here his daddy cry. I swallowed hard as I told him that I hoped to be able to come, though the truth was, I didn't know when I would be able to see him again, let alone watch him practice. I then talked with my younger daughter, which I knew would be the most strenuous due to her and I being the most alike emotionally. True to form, she wept intensely. Tremendously fighting back tears, I tried to console her, telling her it was going to be alright. Though, I myself wasn't even convinced of that. This call was the most gut wrenching thing I've experienced, and when I went back to my cell, I simply broke down; and I wept. I cried bitterly for what seemed to be hours as I pleaded with God to *please* watch over my precious children, and if it be His will, let me return home to them. As I prayed, laying prostate on the floor, there was a light knock on my cell door. I wiped tears from my eyes, and I noticed that it was the same inmate who slid the note under my door earlier, doing the same with another one. He looked at me for a few seconds, and noticed the tears streaming down my face. He gave me a somber nod as if to say, *"I'm so sorry for you."* I forced a smile and nodded in recognition. I read the note and began to weep intensely. The words were as if God Himself was talking to me. It read; *"Brother Luke, God loves you, and has been calling you. Jesus asked you once, 'Luke, do you love me'?"* I continued reading, wiping away tears as I hung on to each word. *"Was your wife your God? God is a jealous God!"* I cried bitterly because I realized that these very words and questions were spoken to me in a dream after this incident with my wife and I happened. I understood now after reading this note, that it was God talking to me then. In this dream, He was telling me I revered my wife more than I did Him, and He was confirming this through this man who wrote this note to me. I began to understand God had me here behind these bars for a purpose; His purpose. No matter how often I cried in sorrow for my circumstances, ultimately, His will was going to be fulfilled.

A few days later an officer came to my cell telling me I had a clergy visit. I got excited because I thought it was my pastor from the church with which I was affiliated. I arrived in the visiting room to see my brother-in-law's mother, who is an Evangelist. She is a strong woman of God, and has a deliverance ministry. We sat, talked through the glass, and read scripture together. She read Psalm 91 to me and the very first verse was also once spoken to me; *"He that dwelleth in the secret place of the most high, shall abide under the shadow of the Almighty."* She wanted to pray with me and wanted me to release the spirit of guilt that she knew I had been carrying since the accident. I pressed my hand against the window where she had placed hers. I felt *such* a flow of God's goodness and grace radiate within the room and felt as though a tremendous burden was being lifted from me. Once more, I wept bitterly. As the next few days elapsed, I began to absorb the Word of God. I studied book after book and chapter after chapter. My soul became gravitated to learn and know more about God. Being locked in my cell for 23 hours a day, left me with only time to meditate on scripture, and the more I read, the more I was shown and taught. I began having visions and dreams, as scripture cascaded like a waterfall. My faith was being increased as I spent hours at a time fervently praying and reading. One day, I received another note from the Christian man across the pod. In it he was saying I must suffer for Christ – to give in to His perfect will. I was astonished and overwhelmed with what else he spoke in this note. He warned, *"This may be hard to hear and understand, but God sacrificed your wife, in order to get your attention. Christ loved you so much, that through this tragedy, you would receive total salvation." Oh!* Tears flowed as these words permeated within me. The thought that God could possibly love me so much that He allowed this accident to occur – just for me. But why? Why me? Why this and why now? I could only think of the life of Job from the Bible, and how God allowed Satan to touch his life knowing in the end it would be for His greater good.

This man's words fixated my heart as I felt God speaking through them. It was very problematic for me to be in jail, and be apart from my family, especially not knowing when I'd see home again. However, I began to form a personal relationship with the Creator of the universe.

It was the weekend before my sentencing day, and I was very unsettled as my soul churned within me. My mind spun as I wondered what sentence the Judge would hand down to me. I reflected back to a word spoken over me one day during a church service when the pastor took me to the front of the congregation and said a miracle was coming my way. I couldn't help but hope and wonder that this was it. Together, my wife and mother came to visit me the day before and did all they could to uplift me. My mother told me that no matter what the Judge says not to worry about it because God has the final word. I spent the rest of the night consumed in prayer, as I pleaded for favor with the Judge.

Monday morning arrived, and my sleep was troublesome. My spirit was vexed throughout the entire night. I began pacing my cell when I looked and saw the escorting officer arrive at my door. I was taken to the first floor lobby where I sat and waited to be taken to court. A female officer approached and asked, *"Have you been to your hearing yet?"* I told her no, and that I was waiting to go. She responded compassionately, *"Good luck."* Another officer approached and asked me to stand as he placed handcuffs and shackles on me. I was escorted by four officers to the courtroom and couldn't help but ponder why it took so many deputies to escort me. We walked the corridors leading to the courtroom. Many employees came to their office doors to catch a glimpse of me, the State Trooper fallen from grace. I then understood all the security. I felt like a death row inmate on display while taking his last steps before his final breath departs him. I felt detached from the world around me as disgust, hurt and shame enveloped.

We arrived at the entrance of the courtroom; the officers removed the cuffs, shackles, and instructed me to remain calm in the courtroom. They advised me to enter and take the seat next to my attorney. The officers opened the door, and it was then that I saw my family and friends sitting there anxiously waiting to see me. I looked to the left corner of the room, and just as the days during the trial, there sat the media with cameras fixated on me. I smiled when I saw a close friend whom I grew up with sitting there. I shook hands with my attorney and took one last glance at my family. They winked; they smiled, and gave me thumbs up as tension filled the courtroom in anticipation of the Judge's entrance. It was hard to fathom that only weeks ago my fate was sealed here in this very room. Now I'm back, with the hope that all that's been spoken over me will come to pass. I'm hoping for a miracle.

The Judge entered, and he instructed my attorney and me to approach the bench. He allowed my wife to speak first and as she approached, I noticed several news media cameras in the corner catching every movement made. I sighed in disgust because I had my fill of them tarnishing and making a stigma of my name.

She cried as she spoke of our relationship and the type of husband I was. I could hear sniffles throughout the courtroom as she spoke tenderhearted words. I listened while she told the Judge about our marriage and about me, and tears whelped in my eyes. She told him I was the kindest man she knew, and I would never do anything to hurt her or anyone else. I was proud of her for standing up for me when others thought her to be foolish for supporting me. Your Honor then gave me the opportunity to do what I hadn't done the entire time since the accident; I spoke. News cameras swung like a pendulum in my direction as I fought for words through tears. I looked the Judge in the eye, and said *"This was an accident."* I spoke of how I was guilty for both my action and reaction, and this is something I'm going to have to live with the rest of my life. I told him, as I pointed back to my wife, *"That woman is not just my wife you're Honor but she's also my companion."* The most loathsome thing about it was I knew the words I'd just spoke weren't true. And deep down, she knew it too. Tears streamed down my face as I pleaded for mercy and compassion; not only for me, but for my wife, children and family. I asked the Judge to *please* not separate me from them. He then allowed the Prosecutor to speak, and his words ripped through my gut. He spoke many lies and deceit, so much so, one of my sister's wrenched herself from the courtroom being so enraged. The Judge then spoke, and his words were harsh. Several times, he spoke the words *"circumstantial evidence,"* which told me that nothing in this entire case was proven by facts. He told of all the letters of support he's received on my behalf, and how researching through my background, even to my childhood, and he found not a single discrepancy. What he said next crumbled me to shear exasperation, as he told me that all of this is overshadowed with the fact of the crime I committed. I was handed a sentence of ten years. I was paralyzed in disbelief. I looked back at my family who were all in tears except for one sister who seemed to know there was a stronger force going on here than any imagined or knew about. I was stunned as my eyes met my wife's; it seemed as though there were no tears; nor sense of hurt nor sorrow. From that moment, I felt as my sister did.

The deputies came to handcuff me, and once more I caught the eye of my childhood friend, and noticed a large tear drop slowly flow down his cheek. That hurt me so intensely – for throughout our childhood days together – I'd never seen him cry.

The trek to the pod was an eternity. As one foot plopped in front of the other, my body felt numb. Inexplicably, a quaint, calming serenity came over me, given that I was told that I was going to spend the next ten years in prison. It was as if God's divine presence was overshadowing me. When I arrived back to my cell, other inmates from the general population were out. They watched me, and they also watched the television news as if wanting to see my reaction to what just occurred. I was motionless. I had nothing left in me to give. I hated the news now. A bunch of preying dogs sniffing for innocent prey to slaughter. Today, I was the meal. I slumped in my concrete cell and thought, *"Ten years!"* I thought there was no possible way I can do this! I instantly thought of my kids – calculating how old they were now, and how old they would be after this time. I wept bitterly. At the moment, I couldn't even pray because I just didn't know what to say. I didn't know what to think. *"God help me! I'm going to prison!"* My thoughts began to run rampant. I thought, *"A State Trooper who was also a prison investigator. I can't go to prison! They'll kill me in there!"* Suddenly I felt Jesus' words on the cross; *"My God, why hast though forsaken me?"* I went to my cell door, with tears still whelped in my eyes when I noticed the Christian Brother at his cell door across from me. He was looking right at me, and straightway a still small voice within me spoke, *"Remember, God is in control."* Each time I went to my door to venture out, he was there – watching my every move. It was as though his existence there was to watch over me; or though it seemed.

Later this same evening my wife and mother came to visit me. I had learned days before the sentencing hearing that they had a minor falling out, and I felt this visit together was more about me than anything else. Both seemed upbeat and in good spirits as they encouraged me not to focus on the time I was given. For once more I was being told that *"God has a plan and purpose for this."* My attorney told my mom I wouldn't leave for prison for about two weeks, which for me was more than enough time for *God's plan* to spring into action. I told my mother that I didn't want to go to prison and was waiting on my miracle. The words of the inmate trustee came back to me, *"You are the miracle."* I watched as they left together, and though I didn't say it, I could feel the tension between them. My mom asked me to call her tomorrow; however, tomorrow never came.

The following morning, an officer appeared at my cell door, and I noticed the patch on his arm read *transportation.* My heart sunk to the pit of my stomach as he said, *"Mr. McCormick, it's time to go."* Squeamishly, I asked *"Where?"* With a slight look of care, the officer replied *"To C.R.C. Prison. I'm sorry man."* He told me we were leaving at this particular time to avoid the media's attention. He had already taken another group of inmates, but wanted to transport me alone. I gathered my small belongings and asked, *"Can I call my wife and let her know?"* Even as the words left my mouth, I knew the answer – *"You know we can't do that."*

We walked out of the cell, and I looked across the pod at my new found friend one last time. I noticed him holding up a note and I pleaded with the officer to grab it for me. In a sheer act of kindness, he walked over to his cell and took the note, though telling me I wouldn't be able to read it until we processed out. This man – this God given angel to watch over me had tears in his eyes as he clasped his hands together while symbolically lifting them to Heaven in one last prayer for me. As sudden fear overshadowed me, I too, had tears forming from deep within.

I was taken to a room, told to strip, and was placed in a black and white pin stripe jump suit like those seen in movies. Shame engulfed me, as I was taken to a depth of humility that I didn't realize existed. I was placed in shackles, chains, and cuffs, and as I shuffled to the garage area of the jail, other inmates who were waiting to be processed watched with percussive calculation of my every move. I desperately wanted to escape the eyes pressed upon me, so I stood in anticipation of the world awaiting me just beyond the garage door when the deputy received a call on his radio. He turned to me with a look of affinity and said, *"I'm sorry Mr. McCormick. I don't know who tipped them off, but the media is here."* Some of the men waiting to be processed must have recognized me from the news as they became indignant with the deputy and said, *"Come on man you know who tipped them off! It was that darn prosecutor! How else would they have known? That isn't even right!"* Suddenly it seemed that the shackles and handcuffs tore into my skin as my body flinched with rage! I was so tired of being on display for the media! A few of the other inmates looked at me with faces filled with empathy and solace – like they knew what was before me just beyond that door. I looked in their faces, and peeked into their souls; someone whose been there. One yelled out, *"Stay strong man, keep your head up."* I was scared and hurt simultaneously, and didn't know what was lying in the path before me. Then slowly – methodically, the deputy opened the door; and once again, the dogs feasted on their prey. There stood a man from a local news station with a camera on his shoulder. All I could think about was my children seeing their father bound in shackles, chains, and a black and white jumpsuit being escorted ceremoniously off to prison, while their friends at school shared the details of their dad being the focal point of the nightly news. What an embarrassment I must be to them! The thought alone made me disgusted with myself, and I wanted to shuffle the whole matter out of my mind. But no matter the effort put forth, reality slapped me in the face as I traipsed into the van. Tears flowed, more so from anger than anything else. One last dig! Just one more wave of embarrassment the prosecutor had to impose upon me by contacting the news media. He wanted the entire world to see; *"The State Trooper, fallen from grace. From Ohio's pride, to utmost shame."* Oh! I was so disgusted! I felt every part of my life up to this moment was tainted and tarnished. To me now, the media was the lowest form of life's' existence, and I meant that with every fiber of my being!

THE BEGINNING

While enroute to the prison, the deputy made every effort to comfort me, though no words existed that could constrain my despair. We passed the highways and roadways that I once patrolled, and now I am left to wonder when I'll travel them again. I felt like I was traveling through a time warp. I already missed home so desperately. The deputy began telling me what to expect once arriving at the prison, and the closer we got the more frightened I became. I remember repeating over and over, *"Jesus – Jesus – Jesus!"* With my eyes tightly squeezed, I rocked back and forth, my chains grinded deeper into my skin, and I wished I could somehow wake from this dream; though my nightmare was ever present before me. I felt the van exit off the interstate as my body shifted from side to side through curves and turns. I opened my eyes, and there we sat directly behind the fence of the prison grounds. I gazed at the razor wire fence and emptiness consumed my soul as all left me. No words, no thoughts; only barrenness filled my inner being.

The deputy pulled the van off to the side before we arrived at the entrance gate. He reached into his shirt pocket and removed the note the man at the county jail gave him. He advised me that he really shouldn't allow this as he slid it to me through the cage separating us. He told me to read it quickly. Though I didn't feel it at the time, the words were appropriate for the occasion.

Now is the time to suffer with Christ. Please give in to God's will, and accept what He is doing. Brother Luke, the

Lord has a plan for you, and you have to trust and believe
in His purpose."

He ended this note by saying, *"Please Brother Luke, suffer this time for Christ."* With tears streaming down my face, I handed the note back to the officer, thanked him for his kindness, and he proceeded on through the gate of the prison. I didn't know what to expect as I was submerged with fear. The deputy pulled onto the prison grounds, and a corrections officer came out of a building and began searching the outer portion of the van. He then opened the side door, looked inside the vehicle, and with no words stared right through me as if I wasn't there. Clearly, at that moment, I knew I wasn't going to be privy to the same regard as at the county jail. This officer slammed the door, and the deputy was told he could proceed forward through the next entryway, which for me was a step closer to my demise.

The shackles on my legs were rubbing hard into my ankles, and the pain was so excruciating that I wanted to cry. I silently prayed for strength as the deputy parked, helped me out of the van and said *"When you go through the first door, do exactly what you're told. Remember, this is a whole new ball game from the county jail. Good luck to you."* No sooner than those words exhaled from his mouth, a corrections officer yelled for me to stand against the wall. I nodded at two other officers as they passed with a gesture as to say hello, but was greeted with snarls, and instantly the words of the deputy resonated in my ears. Sudden fear overcame me as this huge steel door opened, and with it the beginning of the end of freedom; and I knew it.

A loud, obnoxious, overweight corrections officer gruffly said, *"Get in here!"* My instincts kicked in, and I so badly wanted to say, *"Do you know who I am? You can't talk to me that way, I'm a State Trooper!"* But suddenly it struck me, and it was as though I was looking at a mirage of my life. I was filled with anguish and dejection as I realized, *"That's not who I am anymore!"* A sense of sadness and melancholy set within me, and unexpectedly, I fell in a pit of despair and depression. Suddenly, I didn't care what happened to me. When the realization hit me that I wasn't what I once was, I felt all was lost and gone within me.

I was taken into a large room where I noticed numerous brown jump suits. Three officers stood before me and told me to strip as they watched my every move. I knew by now they were told by the deputy who I was, which I felt enhanced their aloofness. As one searched my mouth, my gums, my cheeks, the other two observed, without their eyes departing from me. It was as though I was on display for these men, like a phenomenon they hadn't seen before. Just as it was with the news media, I felt the same knurling on my bones as I stood naked before these men with no place to hide. I choked back tears, as I was told to bend over, and every crevice of my body was searched. I've never sustained such degradation; for sure, nothing compared to this experience. One of the officers threw a brown jumpsuit, a pair of underwear and socks on the floor before me and crudely said, *"Put these on!"* All three just stood glaring at me like at some point in time I had wronged them, and this was their opportunity to exact revenge. I tried to focus on Jesus and my children, but my vision was obscured by the cloudiness of my present circumstances.

I was escorted to the institutional barber where I received a haircut. Ignorantly, I waited for him to ask how I wanted it, but just as they did in my days in the army, he simply began cutting. When he finished, I glanced at him and said *"Thank you,"* as I witnessed coldness from his heart; his only reply was a frigid, hard, blank stare. I was taken to be photographed and I sat looking at the word written in red directly under my picture; *"INMATE."* I sat on this hard, cold bench in the hallway with my head slouched, chin touching my chest. I was so disgusted with myself and full of shame as it seemed only like yesterday that my photo read *"TROOPER – badge # 741."* I've gone from a badge of honor to dishonor, which bore the label of *inmate # 429- 490*. I wanted to crawl in a corner and sob until I vanished away by drowning in my own tears.

Through the initial admission process, I felt as though there was a bull's eye on me as I was escorted by a corrections officer everywhere I went. Other inmates were told to leave areas and offices that I was about to enter, although at this point of the process, I was consumed in a state of agony.

I was taken to see the administrator, who informed me that at this particular prison, the victim of your crime can in no way be placed on your visiting list. For a fleeting moment I forgot where I was as I yelled out *"No way, that's my wife!"* I know the man thought I was crazy because I began to cry right there in his office. I begged and pleaded with him to *please* let her come in, as I explained *"She really isn't the victim – she never was the victim!"* That in itself I know sounded preposterous. With a calm demeanor he said to me, *"I'm sorry sir. She will not be able to visit you here."* Through my continual pleas I could see he was becoming aggravated, and sternly told me, *"There is no way around it."* I completed the rest of my visitation form, though because of the impact of those words, nothing else mattered. I left his office with a mixture of emotions - deeply wounded and impaired through a frustration that I had never felt before. It was then that my journey got worse.

The officer escorting me had stopped to talk with another officer when he abruptly told me, *"Go stand against that wall!"* Already filled with rage and disgust, part of me wanted to lash out with, *"I'm not a dog for you to yell commands anyway you want to! I used to be held to a 'much' higher esteem than you."* But there again were those words, *"used to be,"* and it was that part that hampered any reaction. While they talked their eyes didn't leave me, so I knew I was their topic of conversation. The other officer looked at me and sarcastically asked, *"How much time did you get?"* Quietly, I responded *"Ten years."* Laughing, he said *"A ten pack huh? You should have killed her, then you would have only got seven years."* If there was ever a moment I wanted to put my hands on someone, it was then! Never before have I felt so enraged, and it took all I had to turn my head away from him, and placidly face the wall to which I was standing. All of a sudden, a scripture came upon my heart. Ephesians 6:12;

For we wrestle not against flesh and blood, but against principalities, against powers, against the rulers of darkness of this world, against spiritual wickedness in high places.

I understood this particular guard was being used to torment me, to the depths of him himself not being aware. The officer motioned with his hand for me to follow him as I was again being separated from general population, to a destination I wasn't aware of. We stepped outside of the building, never speaking a word to each other. I remember my thoughts going to my wife, wondering what was going on in her world during this time of what was going on in mine. I wondered if she ever thought of me, if she even cared. Thoughts lingered so deeply within me that my mind was deviated from reality. I felt the warm sun beaming upon my face, and as I listened to the birds singing, I wondered if anyone else noticed the simplicity of it, for it was a beauty I hadn't before recognized. The time I spent in the county jail, the closest I got to the outside world was in asking my mother on the phone *"How's the weather?"* But I had to stop asking because for her to know I was left out from this commodity of life upset her tremendously. I watched as other inmates moved about in areas all around me as we passed each building, the view to me seeming as New York sky scrapers. We passed what I came to realize was the front entrance to the prison and as I noticed the razor wire fence enclosed around it, I couldn't help but wonder when I'd again see the other side. *Oh!* How I pray for the day to walk through that entrance building. We approached a building which had the marking *C-3* on it, and several other inmates hanging around outside seemed to be basking in the glow of my appearance – as though my arrival was foreknown. We entered the building through a large steel door and the officer, pointing to a spot on the floor told me *"Stand right here!"* He conversed with another officer who approached me and asked *"What are you doing in my pod?"* His eyes were unenthusiastic as he simply glared at me, waiting for a response from me. Lost and confused - without an inkling of thought, I responded *"Because I used to be a State Trooper."* Suddenly, it was as though my response sobered his posture, as he caringly said, *"This is a protective custody pod, and though you will be locked down for about twenty two hours a day, you won't have to worry about anything in here."* I asked if I could use the phone to call my mother, knowing the last image she'd seen of me was on the news in a black and white suit. He told me he could not permit that until I had been completely processed into the system. Upon that, he slammed the cell door - the pounding of my heart slamming along with it.

This cell smelled of smoke and filth, and I couldn't believe the contrast between the cell at the county jail and this one. I paced the cell from end to end, pleading for strength and rescue from deep within my soul. I remember thinking *"I'd better make this bunk,"* for fear of getting in trouble, not knowing the rules. I placed sheets on what I presumed was supposed to be the mattress, though it was anything but that. From my face, tears stained spots on the sheets as I struggled to find equanimity to complete the task before me. I wept so; as a new born child fresh from the womb, I searched with tears, nourishment for my despair.

***

I walked to the window and glared at the clouds forming in the sky, feeling the same overcast forming within my heart. I so desperately wanted to talk with my mother, needing to let her know I was alright, though honestly, I wasn't. I began earnestly praying, imploring with God to make a way for me to call. I asked what it was He wanted for me to do, and to *please* deliver me from this burden. I reminded Him of His word, *"I will not put more on you than you can bear."* I had become depleted by the circumstances surrounding me – stripped of any natural ability to stand on my own. At that moment I happened to look up, and an inmate was standing watching me. He leaned over and spoke to me through the open slot on my cell door which was used to slide food trays in saying, *"Are you ok man?"* My eyes full of tears I responded, *"I can't take this! I need to call my mom and wife!"* He looked behind him to ensure the guards weren't watching as he told me, *"Man, you aren't going to call tonight, and probably not tomorrow either."* My heart again became downcast with grief when he suddenly startled me; *"I'll tell you what though. If you want, I'll make the call for you,"* as he turned and walked away. I didn't know anything about this man other than he was a porter in this particular pod who eagerly wanted to help me. My senses as a State Trooper momentarily kicked in, and I began to wonder if I could trust this man with my personal information. But I had such heaviness on my heart which overrode any doubt within me, so I wrote my wife's phone number on a piece of paper he had given me. Thoughts were beginning to forth come within me – a change of sorts, as I would rather have him with this information in his possession, than that of my mothers. And though I wasn't quite sure of its origin, I recognized the shift for what it was.

Abruptly, another inmate appeared at my cell. This was the roughest, meanest looking dude I'd ever seen. He angrily glared at me and said, *"What's your name?"* After telling him who I was, he slammed a food tray on the open flap of my cell door, and seeming to be incensed, he walked away. This inmate had on a tank top, and on his back he displayed a tattoo which explained his stance towards me, which seeing it infuriated me. Across his back were the words, *Arian Brotherhood.* Instantly, I thought *"Lord please have mercy on me and get me out of here."* I stood my ground in the cell as if stuck in concrete and continued to plead with the Creator of the Universe - *"You did it for Peter and Paul when they were imprisoned, so I believe you can do the same for me. Please Lord, do it for me!"*

The guard turned a master switch which seemingly unlocked every cell door other than my own. I watched as other inmates formed a line, gathered their trays, and one by one sat at tables within the pod. I was famished, yet my stomach wasn't able to consume the slightest morsel. All I wanted to do was to call my wife or mother. Through the opening of my cell door, I watched as others ate, emptied their trays, and passed by my cell. Some nodded their heads as if to say hello; others just stared and walked on past. This was a cruel taste of reality that I had never before experienced. My eyes were being opened to the evil ways of man that were previously inconceivable. I moved to the cell window, closed my eyes and once more I wept bitterly. Through my tears, I heard a voice call out, *"Hey man!"* I hastily wiped my face and turned to see the inmate porter standing at the door. Before another word left his mouth I asked *"Could you please call my wife and let her know where I am, and that I'm ok, and I'll call her as soon as I can?"* He replied, *"Yeah man, I told you no problem."* The phones were right across from my cell and I watched as he called. A part of me was trying to see what he did with the piece of paper after dialing, and the other part of me was simply appreciative. With intensity, I watched as he pointed towards my cell as if telling her *"He's right here looking at me."* He sat the receiver on the counter and came to my cell door and said, *"She said to tell you that she loves you, to stand on your faith, and know that God is working in the midst."* Once again, her standardized response was becoming very common. He asked if I had wanted to tell her anything, to which I said, *"Just tell her that I love her, and I'll call her as soon as I can."* As the words parted my mouth, I pondered the fidelity of them. He went back to the phone, and he returned within a few seconds. Again, he said, *"Your wife said to tell you that she loves you, and that's she's doing all that she can for you."* I extended my hand through the cell door and thanked him for making this call for me. We shook hands as he told me to focus on something in order to keep my mind strong and clear because I may be in this cell for a while. He asked if I had any books to read, to which I held up my Bible, and he stated, *"That's all you need,"* and he gave me back the paper with the phone number on it. Again I thanked him, nodded, and he told me he'd check on me later.

—◆—

Darkness began to set in, and I once more began pacing the cell, while I whispered prayers silently within my heart. I plead for mercy, and beseeched the Lord to tell me what to do to have this burden lifted. I exhausted myself with tears. It was then that I remembered the vision I had while in the county jail of the river of blood in a valley and the spirit of God speaking to me about winning souls for His Kingdom. The scripture in the book of (Luke 4:18-19) was placed upon my heart:

The spirit of the Lord is upon me, because He hath anointed me to preach the gospel to the poor; He hath sent me to heal the broken Hearted, to preach deliverance to the captives, and recovering of Sight to the blind, to set at liberty them that are bruised, to preach the acceptable year of the Lord.

I laid in my bunk gazing at the ceiling, as contours of tears streamed from my face into the canal of my ears. I knew there was an undertaking for me to carry out, though at the time I knew not the foundation. This night was prolonged with thoughts of what God had possibly in store for me, and also with thoughts of being absent from my family. Several times I awakened through the night to find myself looking through the bars of the cell window, while thinking of my mother, father, and children. *Oh!* I so desperately wanted to go home! Repeatedly I pleaded with God to pour out His favor and release me from this prison; for Him to do as He did for His disciple Peter, and charge His angel to dictate my path from this place. I bellowed and wrestled within my soul until the breaking of dawn.

27

FATEFUL ENCOUNTER

Abruptly, my attention was shaken by a guard yelling, *"Get up and turn those lights on!"* There were two guards banging on doors from cell to cell, telling guys to get up and turn their cell lights on. It was then too that I realized I made it through my first night in prison.

Without a sound leaving my mouth, I implored the Lord to enable me to speak with my wife and mother today. I peered out the opening of the door, and I observed one of the officers bearing towards my cell. I called out civilly, *"Excuse me sir! Will I be able to make a phone call today?"* Incensed, with disgust piercing his eyes, he sharply said, *"No! You aren't using the phone!"* And with that, he relented and went to the officer's desk. Was his anger solely in knowing who I was, or what I used to be? Or was he entirely crude? Emphatically, I believe both to be true.

After being served breakfast, an officer came and opened my cell door and said, *"Get dressed McCormick, you've got a pass."* Instantly, I got excited, and thought I was finally going to be able to make a phone call home. I left the enclosure of the cell, and felt the buoyancy of liberty, though I soon learned that my meaning or understanding of a pass far exceeded reality. I walked towards the phone when a corrections sergeant standing at the officer's desk scowled at me and said, *"Where do you think you're going?"* Placidly, I replied, *"I'm going to use the phone."* He chuckled, and with a pesky tone he said, *"No you aren't! Not until you have recreation time!"* He reiterated, *"Right now you're going to follow this officer,"* pointing to one of the officers standing there with him.

I soon realized that due to the knowledge of my prior profession within this institution, I was required to be escorted upon every movement on the prison grounds. While trudging along with this officer, no words were spoken, other than when he pointed to a spot and harshly told me to walk next to the grass on the side of the walkway. I again felt the ray of the sun gleam upon my face, and I wanted to cast my head back and capture the moment. We entered a building and the officer said, again pointing, *"Stand next to that pole!"* This room was full of other inmates going through the processing phase, and beyond my initial scan, I felt a legion of eyes studying me. One inmate stepped out of an office, and as another began to enter, the C.O. stopped him and ordered me to go in. This very nice woman told me to have a seat, and after scanning her office I noticed that she was a mental health doctor. I also noticed several inscriptions and pictures which led me to believe that she was a Christian, which to me explained her demeanor and personality as compared to other staff members. She was very kind and polite as she began an inquiry as to my mental health status. She asked very calmly, *"Why do they have you in protective custody?"* I replied with a sense of brokenness, *"Because I used to be a State Trooper."* I was astonished when I saw tears of compassion fill her eyes as she said, *"Oh, bless your heart! You have never been in trouble before have you?"* I said, *"No ma'am."* Then suddenly, I began to cry. In my effort to try and bring it under subjection, the tears flowed. Being very warmhearted, she handed me a box of tissue and told me to take my time. I began to pour my heart out to her. I told her about how my family and I are believing God will perform a miracle. She looked at me softly and compassionately, and said, *"You stand on that, and never give up on your faith."* Before leaving her office, she told me that she will be believing and praying with me. I don't know if it was right, wrong, or indifferent due to my circumstances and because she was a staff member, but, after gathering myself, I shook her hand and told her, *"God bless you."*

I was then escorted to an area where a female nurse stood, who harshly told me, *"Go behind this partition and strip!"* I became very self-conscious because I knew I was going to be examined by a woman. I heard other inmates in partitions next to me who seemed to have no problem with the situation, though for me it was debasing. I entered the partition area, and she had little difficulty grabbing my private area and telling me to *"Cough!"* And just as hasty as she entered, she left saying, *"Now get dressed!"*

When I was escorted back to the pod, I could once again feel the warmth of the sun beaming upon my face. Words can't describe the feeling, as I seemed to feel it as I never have before. Again, no words were spoken between the officer and me, and I could only think of the kindness of the nurse. Upon being placed back in my cell, I silently thanked God for the goodness and kind affection she showed me. After experiencing such respect and regard, and then to be plummeted to such a degree of nothingness was tumultuous. To be frowned upon with such disdain and indifference is a grievous pill to swallow. For the first time while being on these prison grounds, I was made to feel human again, which is strange in itself.

Later the same afternoon, I was lying in bed with my thoughts when a C.O. came and opened my door. He told me, *"Let's go. You're going to see the Unit Manager!"* From my time as a plain clothes officer and from being assigned to two separate institutions, I understood this person to be the one who handles inmates' affairs. When I talked with this man, he seemed to be agitated. His first question to me was, *"Why didn't you tell me you were the plain clothes officer assigned to both the Lebanon and Warren Correctional Institutions?"* Because this was my first time I ever talked with this man, I couldn't comprehend his question, other than he just wanted to assert his authority. After speaking with him for several minutes, he told me that he contacted both of these institutions and spoke with the investigators. He told me that they both spoke very highly of me, and they also told him that it was a shame what happened to me. He asked me how I felt about staying at this institution as what is called a cadre – this is the term used for inmates assigned here. He told me that the Warden was apprehensive about letting me stay here due to my background because it could be detrimental to my health. Inmates usually do not respond favorably to former law enforcement officials. But he told me that the Warden and Central Office decided that it would be better for me to stay at this institution rather than to go to a different institution to fulfill my sentence in protective custody. He advised me that he would be keeping an eye on me, and to speak to him directly if

I had any difficulties. To be honest, I was so numb inside that I wasn't able to retain anything this man said to me. He could have placed me anywhere because it just didn't matter! At this point, all I wanted to do was call my wife and make amends from the deceit I knew that I held inside.

Later this same evening, my cell door popped open and the officer yelled, "*Get ready for chow!*" I was fidgety because this was the first time I would actually be amongst other inmates in general population. I wasn't sure what to do, and I watched as other inmates gathered around tables. When I scanned the pod, I decided to go to a table where three older men were sitting. My thought being that I'd fit in with them. In what seemed very sudden, they all asked how I was doing and it was then that I knew my intuition to sit with them was right. Although I still felt a bit apprehensive in the midst of the atmosphere surrounding me, they gave me a sense of ease, even if only momentarily. I felt stillness within me, a sense of aloofness as I braced myself for someone to ask me why I was there. But that question never came, and it gave me the impression that they already knew. Subdued, I beheld much sorrow, hurt, and anger, as I skimmed across the area of each table, while scrutinizing the pictures of these men's faces. I felt as though I was being exposed to images that I held within myself; and that being the depth of weariness held within a man's soul. What I beheld in the faces of these other inmates, originated in the mirror of my heart that one fateful night. Never before and never since that time have I visualized such pain as I saw while looking into the eyes of these men's hearts.

Prior to eating, I bowed my head and thanked God, not only for the food I was about to receive, but also for allowing me to be out of the confines of my cell. After praying, I looked up and noticed one of the men looking directly at me. He only smiled and bowed his head as if to acknowledge and regard my offer of gratitude for the meal.

On my way back to my cell, I again took a look around the pod at the men with whom I was just acquainted. While I laid in my bunk, I was struck with curiosity as to what they were thinking about me. Did the same wonderment from seeing a State Trooper incarcerated astound them as much as the harsh reality of it did me? I couldn't help

31

but wonder if they held compassion for me as their polite gestures and head nods conveyed. Either way, I thanked God for the opportunity to breathe outside the circumference of this cell. Somehow – someway, the air I took in felt different.

An hour or so later, the C.O. was once again yelling," *Get ready for rec. Stand by your doors!"* I had no idea what was expected. For guidance, I again watched other inmates, so I'd know what to do. The cell doors opened and many of them raced to the phone. Briskly, I fell in line behind them, eagerly wanting to hear a voice from home. Finally, I was able to contact my wife. Uncertain of her frame of mind due to me being transported to prison, I was cautious in explaining to her that she would be unable to visit me here due to her being the victim of my case. With each call being only 20 minutes, after conversing with my wife I quickly got back in line behind the herd of other inmates. I placed a call to my mother. The moment I heard her voice my heart melted, and hastily I found myself struggling to fight back tears. I needed to be strong for her – sound strong for her, though inside I was a son in dire need of his mother's caring touch. In talking with her, I could hear the skirmish within her to do the same for me. All that was within me eventually broke. And like a young boy who just fell off of his bicycle, I came running to my mother in tears begging for a band aide. I cried profusely as I pressed upon her and her ear became a shoulder for me to lean upon. While going through this time of affliction, I've realized that there is nothing like the love of a mother. No matter what I may face in life, she will always be there. I love her so profoundly. After talking with her my strength was depleted. I went to my cell and collapsed helplessly on the bed. I closed my eyes as the pain rigorously ran through me about how badly I wanted to be home. With tears dropping onto my pillow, I drifted off to sleep as the sound of rain brushed against the window.

<hr>

Another day arrived, and I was again awakened to the boisterous voice of the C.O. yelling for everyone to turn their cell lights on. I came to realize that this was an everyday ritual that I'd have to get accustomed to. I went to breakfast this morning when the cell doors popped. I sat at the table with the same group of guys as the previous evening and was startled when they all said, *"Good morning Luke!"* I sat with my tray and bowed my head to give thanks for the meal. And once again, as I looked up this same man was staring me in my face. Only, this time there appeared to be a tear forming in his eyes. I tried to look away, but an insuppressible force was drawing me to him. Though I had no idea what was going on within this man, I wanted to mend the hurt he felt. There is a verse of scripture in the book of Ecclesiastes that reads: *The misery of man is great upon him.* Though not verbally spoken, the pain bellowed through his eyes. And through his tears, I could see the aforesaid misery.

Unexpectedly, the other men at the table left to dump their trays, leaving this man and me alone at the table. I asked as graciously as I could, *"Are you alright?"* As if waiting for this moment, he looked at me and asked, *"Do you think you are cursed for being in prison?"* I told him, *"Not at all my friend. I just think that sometimes God allows tragic things to happen in our lives in order to get our attention."* With tears whelping in his eyes, he said, *"I know that God forgave me, and I know my wife and kids forgave me, but I can't forgive myself."* I was flabbergasted! I found myself in utter silence because oddly enough his wrestling is that of my own. How can I possibly be of aide to him when I'm a hindrance to myself? When I attempted to help this man, I was forced to look into the mirror. A sight that I'm not yet ready to deal with.

Later during this same afternoon a C.O. came to my cell and yelled, *"Pack it up McCormick, you're moving to cell 1100!"* I slowly gathered my belongings, having no idea why I was being moved. After exiting my cell, the officer stood and pointed in the direction of an empty cell with the door already opened. When I entered, I noticed that someone else's belongings were on one of the beds. I began to place my sheets on my bed when I felt the presence of someone behind me. In a moment of awkwardness, no words passed between us, just stern stares into the others' eyes. I reached forth my hand to introduce myself and broke the glacial chill. Before I could say my name, he abruptly cut me off and said, *"Yeah, I know. You're Luther McCormick, the State*

Trooper!" Intensity filled my being, as we momentarily stood face to face. Instinctively, my defense mechanisms were aroused. He glared at me and he said, *"I followed your case on the news, and I was shocked when you got convicted. Especially, with your wife saying it was an accident."* Alleviated by this statement, I sat calmly on the side of my bed as we conversed. He was very informed about me and my case, which caused me to keep my guard up with him. Though he knew much about me, I knew nothing of this man.

In sharing with me his life story, it was evident he's lived a dubious existence. In listening to him, it became obvious to me that our two worlds had nothing in common. I learned that he was one of the biggest drug dealers in the area, about which he dwelt, and this was his third stint of incarceration. He told me that he was a crack cocaine dealer, *"rock"* as he called it. Ironically, he said he got busted when he attempted a sell to an undercover police officer. All that I could think about was, *"Lord what have you gotten me into by making me cell with this man?"* It was as though he visualized my mind because almost instantly, after this thought, he said to me, *"You know they did this on purpose, right?"* I asked, *"They did what on purpose?"* He said, *"Putting us in this cell together."* He continued, *"Think about it man. Here I am, a career criminal, all my life I've sold drugs and ran from the police. And now, they put me in the cell with one!"* Finally, after a few seconds of thought, we both laughed hysterically! I had to admit that in my 9 ½ years as a State Trooper, this was an experience I'd yet to delve into.

This man told stories that I'd only heard or seen on television. But what was so astonishing to me was the fact that no part of me judged him or his lifestyle. I mean, here we were, two men utterly from the other side of the tracks, yet we managed to thrive through this adversity.

In telling him about myself, I told him I'd be amiss if I didn't mention how God is the rock of influence in my life. I told him how God has kept my mind through this, even when I honestly thought that I was going to lose it. I noticed that the more I spoke about God, the more it seemed to peek his interest. It was as though a door in his heart had been opened for me to step in and minister of sorts to him. I thought back to my time in the county jail when the Holy Spirit spoke to my heart about winning souls for His Kingdom. I felt this could possibly be the soul spoken of, as he seemed to listen intensely, and gravitate to each word I spoke.

With each day that passed, this man and I shared intimate details of our lives. In talking about God's goodness and His love, we would sit and I would read scripture to him. After a few days of this becoming commonplace, I began noticing that he had stopped cursing. I smiled one night when, as he laid with his arm across his head, he said softly, *"Lord, have mercy."* One very late night, he surprised me when he asked if we could do something a little different. Tonight, he wanted to read the Bible to me. After reading a few verses from Job, he stopped and asked, *"Why does my heart feel so dirty?"* He said, *"I'm thirty years old, and I've had only one job my entire life! All I've ever done is wrong!"* I took the Bible from his hands, and I went to Jeremiah 6:13:

> *For from the least of them even unto the greatest of them, everyone is given to covetousness; and from the prophet even unto the priest, every one dealeth falsely.*

I said to him, *"None of us are perfect; we all have sinned and fallen short of His glory. We all have made mistakes. But, through God's grace and mercy, He can deliver us from it all."* I watched as he tumbled back onto his pillow, and his eyelids delicately dipped over his eyes. I witnessed a single tear trickling down the slope of his cheek.

Most mornings, while he slept, with my knees pressing into my bunk, I would turn towards the window and silently pray. This became my sole time of solitude, and a depression blanketed my existence because my mind could only dwell on being home. Time passed, and each day he would tell me of the exploits of his life and of prison life. I would tell him of my love for my family and of God. We were so different. He seemed to crave the only lifestyle he's ever known, while I yearned for the voices and faces of my family. Though family conversations were daily, still, the fact remained that our separation left me hollow. One Sunday morning after breakfast, the yearning really got to me, and before he returned to the cell, I couldn't hold it; I wept uncontrollably. It seemed but a moment, and he came in behind me. Though he observed my tears, I quickly dried my eyes and composed myself.

He shuffled to the window, looked at me and said, *"Come here Luke."* Rain was falling as he said, *"Stick your arm out the window."* He noticed the strange look on my face, and he said to me, *"Trust me."* I slowly and intentionally slid my sleeveless arm out the window and I experienced and observed the cool rain drops dance on my skin. He then told me, *"Now close your eyes, and listen to the sound of the birds."* I suddenly succumbed to a sense of solace and solitude, and he said to me, *"God is in everything."* He gazed at me with eyes of sincerity and serenity, and confessed about how he's enjoyed the pleasant peace he received when I placed God's word on him daily. He explained to me that God spared his execution and it wasn't just circumstance or coincidence that united us. Instead, our unlikely encounter was orchestrated by the King to soften my heart and transform his soul. He told me that God graciously spared his life on several occasions. He said he was shot and stabbed twice while peddling drugs. He told me a story of how his car was also stolen, and when he and his cohorts caught the carjackers, he found himself looking down the barrel of a shotgun. He said that when he feverishly fled, his shoulder was exploded by a shotgun blast, and while lying there partially unconscious, he could hear three men converse as they hauntingly hovered over him.

He recalled one man's utterance, *"Man, kill this dude! Blast him!"* He heard a round being chambered into the shotgun, and an empty casing tumbled to the ground and landed next to his head. With tears of fear and anguish forming in his eyes, he said, *"I just knew that I was dead. But for whatever reason, they suddenly ran away!"* When I heard this incredible story, I was moved to tears. When our eyes met, I told him, *"It sounds as though there were several times in your life that you could have died, but your life was spared. Do you ever wonder why?"* He said, *"Yes. I'm wondering that even now."* I told him, *"Man, look at us! A State Trooper and a drug dealer sharing a cell in prison together!"* He giggled through the onset of tears and said, *"God truly works in mysterious ways."* I told him, *"I believe that God spared your life for such a time as this."*

I watched him lie back on his bed and drift into a deep and peaceful slumber. By reliving his story, or the memory of it, it depleted his ability to remain awake.

I edged onto the side of my bed and just gazed at the sweltering walls surrounding the cell. A sudden breeze swept through the window, and I caught the scent of freshly cut grass. I peered out the window and saw inmates cutting grass across the grounds of the institution. *Ah!* The smell was divine! I slowly and gently closed my eyes and pondered the beauty and wonder of God's marvelous creations. I thought about how throughout my life that I've taken so much for granted - like the simple scent of freshly cut grass. My experience has created a sensitivity and awareness of creation unlike ever before, and I was rendered incapable of preventing my wonderment about what this grass would smell like if I were home – if it would be the same as now. At that moment, all I wanted was to ingest the fragrance of the freshly cut grass from the front lawn of my father's house. My childhood playground.

———◇———

One early evening during rec time, I had a very toilsome phone conversation with my mother. I explained to her how my heart was so saturated and overridden with remorse and guilt for imposing such shame to my family. A current of tears strolled down my face as with a gentle and sensitive tone she said, *"Luke, no one is ashamed of you. Not your wife, your kids, not anybody. Don't you even begin to think that."* I loathed my existence for the anguish my family now endures each day of their lives. For my lapse in judgment and my infringement of the choice I made that night, by reason, their existence too, has been fixed.

Upon concluding the heartrending call with my mother, I hastily withdrew myself from the phone. My most foreboding fear was for the incoherent utterances of my tears to be gawked at by other overly curious inmates. I traced around the pod, and was drawn to a window, in an attempt to restrain the unnecessary embarrassment of tears. I looked attentively at the imposing razor wire fence engulfing the institution. A yearning to be free was ratcheted into my soul, as time stopped and my present reality suffocated the belief that I would ever be in the comfortable confines of home.

After rec, laboriously I lumbered back to my concrete hell, and my cell mate once again asked if I would read the Bible to him. I softly chuckled as I perceived that his heart was being transformed. He sat quietly and attentively, and at one point he said to me, *"Luke you'd make a good Sunday school teacher."* Then he truly startled me when he told me, *"You are going to be famous one day Luke. I don't know how, but God is going to use you."*

Lying with my head buried in my pillow that night, I pondered on what he had told me. Each night as I slept in the cell with this man, I wondered if God would truly use me in some form or fashion. Honestly, I wondered if I was counted worthy enough to be used by God. When he talked about of his times of incarceration, I've learned through him that prison life can consume a man's mind, along with his body. I know that I have cried a dreadful number of tears, but intermingled between each tear was God's spirit to anchor my sanity.

I woke early the following morning and I went to gaze out the window. I again witnessed the beauty and splendor of God's creations as I watched the sun rising above the tree line which encompassed the prison grounds. I was suddenly pummeled and immersed with thoughts of reality. *"I can't believe I'm here. I don't belong here!"* I reflected on my confinement and I thought it to be so unjust. I perceived myself to be different among these other inmates. In my heart and my soul, I knew that I was different. Though my surroundings, all spoke otherwise, because here I stood nestled amongst them. From this window, I could see the Sheriff's deputy cars transporting inmates through the back gate of the institution. All the while I thought, as each patrol car entered, *"That's the flock of people to whom I should be joined. That's, where I belong!"*

Later this same afternoon, after eating lunch, my cell mate asked me to read him a short story in the Bible. I know he typically sleeps throughout the day due to the lifestyle which he lived, and as he laid back with his arms cuddled beneath his head, I read to him the short story of the book of Ruth. I marveled, as I watched him drift off to a peaceful slumber. I closed the Bible and was immersed in deep thought as I reflected back to my time in the county jail. I recall the man who sent letters to my cell. He once told me that God wanted me to focus on His word. I realized that by reading daily to my cell mate that I was acquiring a personal relationship with my Savior. In the midst of assisting in the mending of his heart, I too, was being healed.

⸺◈⸺

Later that afternoon I read a loving letter I had received from my mother. It generated a stream of tears which cascaded down my face. I believe my cell mate could hear the clamorous secretion of emotion being brought forth out of me because at one point he rolled on his bunk with his back facing me, leaving me to be private with my tears. My heart gleamed as my mother told me how proud she always was to have me for a son, and how this situation in no way changes that.

When I read the letter from my sister, she told me about going to her church and hearing a well-known bishop speak. She told me how his message made her think of my condition. She recounted how the bishop said, "*Take if you will the making of a man, as you go through you're fiery tests and trials. You'll come out as pure gold!*" She said, as she listened intently to his message, she equated what he was saying to the trials and tribulations that are ever present before me. In her letter she wrote, "*Lukie, read Job 23:10.*" I quickly clutched my Bible and read this verse.

> *But he knoweth the way that I take: When he hath tried me, I shall come forth as gold.*"

What I also found astonishing was that just a couple of days prior to receiving the letter from my sister, my cell mate had just read portions of Job to me. My sister also said that this bishop spoke about how God will hide Himself from you, as to not look upon your sins, in order to see what you will do. In a flash of thought, I was reminded of a scripture I knew in Isaiah 57:17, 18:

39

> *For the iniquity of his covetousness was I wroth, and smote*
> *him: I hid me, and was wroth, and he went on frowardly*
> *in the way of his heart. I have seen his ways, and will heal*
> *him: I will lead him also, and restore comforts unto him*
> *and to his mourners.*

In a dream, it was shown to me that God hid His face from me, because He has taken notice of all of my improprieties. But it was also shown that He had forgiven me for it all, and was healing me. I believe that despite the entanglement of this affliction, my time of incarceration is a source of healing for me – that *"making of a man!"*

I stood gaping out the window as I wrestled with the words of my sister the remainder of the night. I became lost in my thoughts as the chirping melody of crickets fascinated me. I thought of my mother and sister, and how I relish in their love and care for me. I thought of my children, and how I've longed and yearned to be a role model for them. Yet, here I stand, gazing out this window, immersed in deep thought. I fell into a passive slumber, and exuded tears until they trickled into the desires of my dreams of one day being home.

⬗◆⬖

As the days sluggishly proceeded by, my cell mate and I became more entrenched in studying the Bible. We also became more intuitive of the makeup of each other. Constantly, I was amazed at how two men who are so diverse in kind and character could abide together in such a dwelling as these four walls. Submerged with this thought, my cell mate said to me, *"Read to me the story of Joseph."* It seems that the word of God places a soothing peace upon my cell mate, because once again as I was reading, he lethargically fell into a stupor. Silently, I read, and as I did, I thought about how aspects of my life are like Joseph's. The same way that he ran from the lustful grasps of a woman, in essence, is parallel to my longing to be severed from the grip of inelegance. In the story of Joseph, he was confined due to the lies and betrayal of a woman. My constraint was the fraudulence of my own self-control, which invariably imprisoned me. I thought about me running the night of the incident. I feel as though I've been running my entire life. I am impoverished and wanting because of the despair of failed relationships that's besieged me.

Unexpectedly, the C.O. came and opened our cell door and said, *"McCormick, you have a visit!"* I attempted to quickly neutralize my mind and permit the passage of translucent thoughts of my family. The sun dispensed it's warmth on my skin, and I felt a youthful burst of vitality, with the anticipation of seeing my loved ones. As I walked about the compound, it gave me a temporary feeling of existence. As the officer escorted me across the confines of the institutional grounds to the visitation building, my lungs began to breathe in and expel the warmth of the lustrous air. Upon entering the visitation room, being subjected to a strip search had no effect on me because I was overcome with a sudden surge of excitement. I knew that soon, the embrace of my mother would engulf me. However, the officer then told me that due to being on separation status, my visit would have to be in the *"cage."* This is a small room comparable to that of the county jail. Once more, I'd have no physical contact with my family. Likewise, in this enclosure, my heart would savor the distant embrace of my mother.

Upon entering the room, and just as it was on my first visit at the county jail, there sat my mother, my baby sister, and my brother-in law with glistening smiles on their faces. I clutched the receiver on the wall and my heart dissolved in my chest when my mother said to me, *"I thought I was going to get to hug you!"* Oh! How I missed her! I was heartbroken, and felt liable for the anguish she carried within her. I also felt that due to the tort of my judgment, she too, was being punished. Through her radiant smile and the gleam in her eyes, my mother tussled with being deprived to embody the display of affection that we both longed for. I peered over my mother's shoulder and could see other inmates gaping inside the room at me. It was a mirror image of the news media as they gawked at me. It was as though they knew who I was, or what I used to be, because they seemed to describe in detail the image I once represented to their families.

My sister sat perched in her chair with her eyes fixed on me with an immense smile on her face. She broke her silence, and said, *"You look good!*" In an attempt to be encouraging, my brother-in-law began to tell me about a story he had read recently in the Bible, but couldn't recall the passage. He said it was a story of a man who was thrust into prison, then was delivered, and became an exceedingly great man of God. Almost simultaneously, my mother and I both said, *"That's the story of Joseph!"* I marveled as I told him that I had just read that story to my cell mate. It was then that I apprehended the discernment of my brother-in-law using the story of the plight of Joseph to aide in a better understanding of my precarious circumstance.

Because I was not permitted food while on my visit, my family restrained themselves from using the vending machines in the visiting room. I knew they were becoming famished and weary, so I pleaded with them, and convinced them that I'd be okay and that they needed to go. So, after indulging in the vigorous delight and pure gratification of my family, they departed with my mother showering me with blown kisses. I watched as they walked away, and I ached to leave with them. Yet, I was left alone in the cage with torment and anguish in my heart.

Later that same evening, during rec time, I placed a call to my wife. An instance of sadness persisted over me because she was unable to come. Yet, I was still being overwhelmed with exuberance of seeing my family, and wanted to share in that with her. However, out of guilt I couldn't muster the strength, and tucked those emotions within myself to savor for a lasting time. Oh how I missed them already.

⬦

One night, while I was settled in my bunk, resting from the exertion of the many thoughts that have traversed my mind. My cell mate, seemingly shuttered, and abruptly sat straight up in his bunk. He looked directly at me and said, *"I had a dream that everyone was mean to me, and was mistreating me. I was talking to my father about it, and we both were crying."* With his head shrouded between his knees, I sensed that this dream tormented him and left him distraught. He asked me, *"What does this mean?"* Hushed, I delicately sat up on my bunk and faced him and said, *"God is changing your heart. And in that process, those who have* known you all of your life may oppose you, and that includes your family." He hastily left his bunk and walked over to the sink and said, *"How did you know it was my family in the dream?"* I replied, *"I didn't."* He stood glaring in the mirror as if he was scrutinizing the image glaring back at him. He said soberly, *"I don't know what I would do without you Luke. You have been such a blessing to me."* He alighted back onto his bed with his shoulders slumped and his chin tumbled to the top of his chest. A stillness filled the compass of the cell, and an intensified silence appeared to fill his heart. He spoke quietly, *"I'm institutionalized Luke."* I asked him, *"What does that mean?"* He said, *"I've been in and out of prison. I don't know anything else."* And with that, he closed his eyes and drifted into a peaceful slumber.

As the dawn arose, I noticed that he was already awake. He was staring at me like a child abiding in the anticipation of his parents rising. As I raised myself from the bed, he modestly said to me, *"God used you to touch my life. All of your training as a State Trooper could never have prepared you for this time. You never judged me, but you guided me. I have to be honest with you. When I first came to this cell with you, I tried to intimidate you because I didn't want to cell with a cop!"* He chuckled, *"God sure has a sense of humor."* I was ambushed when he spoke about intimidating me, but it made me recognize that God's protective hand has been with me. Never once did I sense his intention to intimidate me. Deflated, he continued, *"Luke, show me the way to peace and salvation. As far as I'm concerned, you are my minister, and I love you. Show me how to live like you."* I grasped my Bible and read to him 1 John 1:9;

> *If we confess our sins, he is faithful and just to forgive us our sins, and to cleanse us from all unrighteousness.*

I then said to him, *"It's simple. You only have to believe."* We clutched each other's hand as we placidly tumbled to our knees and bowed our heads in subdued humbleness. I guided him, as he implored the Creator of the universe to forgive him of his transgressions, and to save his soul.

These were the last words that we spoke to each other because later that same afternoon, I was transferred to the cadre pod. As the sergeant yelled for me to pack up my things, my cell mate said to me, *"It's time."* We embraced, and with the silhouette of tears forming in his eyes, he looked at me and said, *"I love you Luke. I really do."* With that, I departed from the protective isolation of solitude, and into the world of the general population.

GENERAL POPULATION

I reported to my new pod, and as I entered, I was met by a C.O. who directed me to a cell which was in a corner on the top tier of the pod. Other inmates were gathered throughout, some shooting pool; others playing cards, but all were watching me. A sudden fear overwhelmed me, and with each step I traipsed, it was as though I could hear the undertones of, *"That's the State Trooper from the protective dorm."* As I entered the cell, I had to find enough might to suppress the tears that were forging their way to my eyes. I imagined that the top bunk would be my domicile, given that it was vacant of linens. Just as I began to unpack my belongings, another inmate walked into the cell. He had a very calm demeanor as he introduced himself and said, *"I'm your cellie. Make yourself as comfortable as possible in here. If you need anything let me know."* He told me that he had to go back to work but for me to make myself as comfortable as possible, which left me alone with the harsh climate of my surroundings. I didn't know what to do. I was lost in an atmosphere for which I wasn't prepared.

After a while, I placed a call to my children because I hadn't spoken to them since my time at the county jail. I urgently longed to hear the word *daddy* from their adorable little voices. My younger daughter answered the phone, and as soon as she heard my voice she wept. My heart instantly dissolved. To hear my precious little girl cry rent every fiber in me and left me destitute and dejected. While gulping and digesting her anguish, I tried to alleviate her sufferings by saying to her, *"Daddy will be home soon."* Though veritably, I had no firm conviction of that reality. I just knew that in some way daddy had to quiet her tears. I then spoke with my son, and I chuckled as he gave me an update on all of the pro wrestling news. I did all I could not to deviate from this topic and kept it as the center of our conversation. I couldn't bear hearing him ask, *"Daddy, when are you coming home?"* Eventually, I spoke to my oldest daughter. Her first few words to me were, *"Daddy, I remember our promise."* Though I know that she was hurting too, she felt honored to look after her younger siblings. Even through her youthfulness, I cherished her strength. Individually, I told each of my children how I loved and missed them so immensely. The hurt I heard in the voices of my children penetrated and severed my core. The magnitude of my indiscretions has brought extreme grief to their pure innocent lives.

I then placed a call to my mother. In telling her about the conversation with my children, she confessed to me that though she had initially kept it from me, my kids were having a very hard time dealing with my incarceration. In particular, my youngest daughter was struggling. She said to me, *"She's always felt the closest to you, and she feels like you've left her."* In hearing that, the distillation of my tears poured forth like a raging current. With her motherly gentleness, she tried to comfort me by saying, *"Luke, it's going to be okay. Your kids are going to be alright, because God is in control of this."* I stood in the phone station, and loathed my existence. I wept bitterly.

———◆———

As the evening approached, I was trying to get acquainted with the confines of my new cell and cell mate. He and I talked briefly about our lives, and I learned that he was in prison due to committing murder. I learned from my prior cell mate that it's deemed disrespectful to discuss, or ask questions of other inmates regarding their reason for incarceration. However, he and I discussed things openly, as if to show the other that we had nothing to conceal. Coincidentally, this seemed to bring about a mutual respect and understanding toward him and me. He made me aware of the day to day general operation of prison life as a cadre. I learned that almost every inmate is assigned a job, and he informed me of the times you had to be in your cell for count, which is when the C.O. in your pod goes cell to cell and ensures that all inmates are accounted for. Through the discussions we shared that night, I concluded that he is one of the nicest guys to whom I've ever been acquainted.

As the night drifted leisurely on, all thoughts of a tranquil sleep escaped me. I was troubled, and immersed in Scripture which cascaded over my mind. I closed my eyes and reflected on the many nights that my former cell mate and I read Scripture together. This particular night while lying prostate on my back, I reflected on one of those verses. Lamentations 3:26;

> *It is good that a man should both hope and quietly wait*
> *for the salvation of the Lord.*

I closed my eyes and determined that God is my hope, and I know that He will deliver me from the affliction of oppression.

The following morning, my cell mate left early for his job in the kitchen. I paced within the cell and waited for count to clear. While waiting, I tuned his radio to a gospel station, and found myself worshiping with adoration to the goodness of God.

During the afternoon, I was told to report to the unit manager's office for my job assignment. I was told by other inmates that more than likely I'd be assigned to the kitchen because that's where all the new cadre is initially assigned. I entered the office area, and while waiting to speak with the unit manager, I engaged in a conversation with another inmate who was also waiting for a job assignment. While talking with him, I learned that he has spent most of his adult life in prison, and that this was his fourth term of confinement. I tried not to be evident as I shook my head in disbelief. He apparently perceived my thoughts because he said abruptly, *"This time, I have come to the realization that's its only God who can change me."* His statement opened a brief dialog. I said to him, *"So many people facing challenges and issues in life think that they can change themselves, only to fail. But just like the realization that you have come to, it's God who changes the hearts of man."* As we conversed quietly, we became a little more knowledgeable about each other when together we were called into the unit manager's office. I was astounded when the unit manager knew this inmate by name, and also made mention of his brother being incarcerated here. Instantly, I thought, *"How must their mother feel?"* I thought of my own mother, and the anguish she feels for her only son being incarcerated. I know the distress she battles daily – hourly, so I can't fathom the affliction of a mother having two sons confined. In the little time that he and I spoke in the hallway, he was disinclined to dole out his brother's incarceration.

We were simultaneously instructed by the unit manager on the rules and regulations expected to be carried out by cadre inmates. Before asking him to step out he said to us, *"One of you are going to the kitchen, I just haven't decided which one."* But then, as he closed the door behind the other inmate, he told me, *"I just said that for his benefit. There's no way I'd send you to the kitchen over him, especially with your background. The warden said that even though you're in general population, I have to keep you away from all the disarray and chaos as much as possible. I have to put you somewhere that I can keep an eye on you."* He then told me that he was going to place me in the commissary, which he stated is a job assignment that other inmates would love to have. All that scampered through my mind was that this was *God's favor.* He told me, that if I desired, in a couple of years, I could transfer to another assignment. But with that, I said to myself, *"It doesn't matter. I'll be home soon."*

——◆——

After leaving his office, I went back to my cell only to find my cell mate and three of his friends there. I told them about my job and simultaneously they said, *"Man! You are lucky! Nobody new goes anywhere other than the kitchen, especially not to a job like the commissary."* I thought of what the unit manger had said just moments ago, and again was immersed in the thought of God's benevolence. After getting over the impact of not being assigned to the kitchen, one of them began expressing to me that even before my arrival, staff and inmates alike were conscious of me coming here. He said to me, *"In all the years and stints that I've been locked up, no one has caused such a stir or brought such fascination or intrigue like you. Everyone is talking about the State Trooper!"* One of the other men said, *"Yeah. This is my third number, and I haven't seen anything like the day you got here."* He chuckled and said, *"No offense, but you are like a celebrity man."* I was utterly amazed at the stories these men told.

Of the many prisons they have been in and out of - and this seemingly being a normal way of life for them - like the life of reformatory is the most natural sense of familiarity that they've invariably understood. It sounded as though they were describing college campuses as they spoke about the many different prisons they have frequented. But what I found extremely amazing was that through their ineptness and lack of sense or reason, and their coarseness and vulgarity emerged men of decency. Veritably, I appreciated their regard.

Later that evening, I was able to go out and walk the track which encompasses the recreation yard of the institution. Things appear to me so differently now. I gazed at the wooded area that is just outside the fence which encompasses the prison. I felt as though I was examining and exploring exhibits of natural creation that I was seeing for the first time. The birds, trees, and the clouds, are all a wonder to me now. Being in prison has caused me to cherish things such as I never have before. But more than anything, I yearn for the savory taste of freedom. I had no notion or thought about the atmosphere of inmates which encircled me. As I walked, I meditated upon the Scripture I heard the woman at the county courthouse softly sing while she entered the elevator; *"No weapon formed against me shall prosper."* Though I sensed and understood that most eyes were fixated upon me, I also believed that God's protective covering was with me as well.

The following morning, I was overcome with elation when the C.O. called my name for a visit. I was so ecstatic and excited to see my family! When I entered the visitation room, I virtually collapsed in the loving arms of my mother. This was the first physical contact I have been able to have with her since the week of my trial. Like the feeling of a little child; O*h!* How I've longed to be cuddled in her embrace! One of my sister's and brother-in-law were also present. As we embraced, and because this was my first time being in the midst of this atmosphere, I scanned the confines of the visitation room. My mother asked, *"Do you want a cold soda?"* My lips quivered, like being depleted of thirst as eagerly I replied, *"Please!"*

AN UNCOMMON FRIENDSHIP

The following Monday morning I started my job at the commissary. I was extremely nervous because I didn't know what to expect or how the other inmates would react to me. I spoke with the supervisor and learned about my duties, and then was introduced to the other six inmates with whom I'd be working. To my dismay, I stood face to face with the inmate from the protective custody pod who bore the *"Arian Brotherhood"* tattoo. Sternly, he glared at me, in a futile attempt to coerce me into intimidation. Seconds of silence passed before we simultaneously extended our hands and gave a head nod gesture of greeting. During a break from filling inmates store orders, I approached him as he stood alone at the front counter. For reasons, I could not explain due to our first encounter, I was drawn to this man. He spoke with an extremely gruff tone, yet unexpectedly, I found myself engaged in conversation with him. He didn't acknowledge my background as a former State Trooper, as I didn't acknowledge his Arian Brotherhood following. As the next few days and weeks expired, he and I became more amicable about conversing with one another. Within the pod, I learned that the majority of black inmates avoid this man due to the nature of his following. Albeit, these same inmates also disassociate themselves from me due to my background. It's almost as though they see a link between me and why they're in prison, as if in some way

I played a hand in their being incarcerated. The same way inmates and staff alike look at me with wonderment is the same perception he bears due to his affiliation. It was really strange at times how he and I communicated. Our discussions were very coarse and raw. We left nothing to the imagination as everything was laid on the table. One day he even asked if I understood now how it feels to be on this side of the law. He must have seen the startled look in my eyes because before I had a chance to respond almost in an apologetic sense he told me that he was not trying to be a smart butt, but I could see now how things really are when you're being mistreated and made to feel like you're a piece of trash under someone's foot. Though personally, I haven't experienced or received treatment to the extent he spoke, I had to admit that as an inmate you are viewed as a lower class citizen. I know that, deservingly so, I'm being punished for my life's choices. However, I truly wish that this stint of incarceration was a punishment I didn't have to endure.

On another occasion during a conversation he and I were engaged in, he told me about a day when another inmate approached him and was indignant concerning me. He said that he told him he has noticed him talking to me lately and wanted to know what I was like and about. He told me that he told this other inmate that he didn't know any cop! He told him that he knows a man named Luke! He said that he then told this guy that I was actually a cool dude once you got to know me. He then told me that as far as he is concerned, we are all inmates, no matter what we were on the streets.

I know that a lot of these inmates look at me and judge me because I was a State Trooper. But this man was different. Ironically, he seemed to take it as a personal initiative to keep an eye on me, and let others know the difference as well.

Later this same evening while working out in the gym, I was approached by a short and very stocky older guy. He had the look of a very hard, callous individual who has spent several years behind the confines of prison walls. He said to me, *"What's up slim? I see you are over there getting it in."* After a short banter, he said unhesitant, *"Look bro, it's no secret as to who you are. As soon as you stepped on the grounds of this institution everyone knew that the State Trooper was here"* A word barely left my breath before he continued, *"Don't even worry about it dog. You'll be alright!"* Then intentionally, and of his own volition, he began to openly tell me about his case. He told me that he is fifty seven years of age and has been in prison for seventeen years after being charged with double murder for the killing two men in self- defense. I stood flabbergasted, being unable to speak but a few words. Our oral exchange ended with him telling me, *"No matter what I do, or how things look; don't ever give up!"* I can only take humor in the fact that the criminals who seemingly had the toughest exterior have in some way befriended me.

One morning when I was working at the front counter of the commissary, an inmate knocked on the window to get my attention. When I looked up, I recognized him as the same guy who worked as a porter at the county jail, and who slipped notes to me from my Christian friend. I gathered my thoughts and quickly recollected that he had gone home prior to my departure from the county jail. He had an extremely somber look on his face as he looked at me through the thick Plexiglas window which separated us. Softly, with his lips he gestured the words, *"Please pray for me. I got four years."* I didn't ask him why he received a four year sentence, though desperately within the question lingered, *"What are you doing here?"* As he moved down the counter of the commissary line our eyes never departed from each other. I couldn't fathom what could have possibly gone array for him to now be in prison after only a few months of being home. After receiving his items, he leaned down to an opening in the window and said, *"Seeing you here makes my prison stay much easier to deal with. It's been worth my while just seeing you. God bless you brother."* And with that he departed, and our paths never again crossed. My face to face encounter with this man brought a whole new perspective on the word *freedom* to me that day. When I saw him, I understood that without God guiding my every step, I too, could once again tumble into the pitfalls of life's circumstances. These same circumstances ultimately led to my own personal path of ruin. This day when I saw that man, I realized that I would do whatever is required for me to never again return to what brought me here.

The following morning, when again working at the commissary, I observed two men dressed in suits approaching the entrance. The instant I laid eyes upon them I knew who they were as did the other inmates working with me. These men were what I once was; plain clothes investigators with the Highway Patrol. What was even more disheartening was that one of the Troopers was a friend of mine.

As they entered into the commissary, the C.O. escorted them to the supervisor's office. They passed directly by the area where I was working, but neither of them made any form of eye contact with me, nor ventured a glance in my direction. With anguish elevating within me, I too avoided all points contact. Surprisingly, my new found Arian Brotherhood friend angrily asked me if I was alright. I told him that I was, but their presence infuriated me. They reminded me of everything that I once was, and somehow I felt this was the purpose of their visit. One of the other inmates stated, *"I think maybe that one of them is a new Trooper and the other one is showing him around."* My friend boldly told him that they were just trying to rub it in my face! I felt the intense sensation as tears began to fill my eyes. The C.O. inconspicuously and empathetically nodded towards me as if to say, *"I'm sorry."* I believe that he sensed that I was outraged and hurt beyond reason. Eventually, I could hear the supervisor's office door open, and he escorted the two Troopers towards the front entrance of the commissary. As they passed, the one whom I once thought to be my friend looked in my general direction before dropping his head. I thought, *"This is a man who I not only rendered aide to when he first graduated from the Patrol Academy, but he's also someone who spent time in my home. And now, whether the source was from shame or empathy, he couldn't bear to look me in the eye."* I quietly stood still, and watched as they walked towards the front entrance of the institution. Suddenly, a large and heavy thump landed on my shoulder with a voice that followed. *"Forget about them Luke! They aren't nothing compared to you."* Once again, I was being comforted by an inmate who befriended me. With a decisive and unwavering glare, he said to me, *"Look at me! You keep your chin up! They aren't nowhere near the man that you are!"* It overwhelmed me that once again here is a man of a completely contrary background to that of my own liberating me in a time of need.

Later that morning, I had to go back to the pod for count time. I was so overridden and overcome with emotion that I literally crumbled prostrate, with my face pressed to the cold concrete floor. I wept bitterly.

When I returned to work for the afternoon, I was greeted by the supervisor who directly called me into his office. He appeared to be suffocated by his emotions, and upon closing his door he calmly said to me, *"I'm so sorry Mr. McCormick. Sir, I thought one of those Troopers was showing the other one around the Institution and wanted to talk to me about the operation of the commissary."* With a somber look he continued, *"They tricked me. They just wanted to see you; they simply wanted to see you in prison. I'm truly sorry. I can only imagine how you must feel."* As tears formed in my eyes, he continued profusely to utter how bad he felt. He also told me that it upset him so much that he had to call his wife to help calm his nerves. He said, *"I cannot believe that they would want to actually gloat like that! In all of my fifteen years working in this institution, I've never seen anything like that!"* He never told me exactly what was said by the two Troopers, but it was enough for their intentions to be made known. Prior to leaving his office, I thanked him for his honesty, care, and concern. The C.O. working the commissary then took me aside and apologized as well. He said that he was told the Troopers were taking a tour of the compound and wanted to visit the commissary. He told me that if he had known their intentions that he would not have given them access to the store. It was very difficult for me to comprehend that a profession which I once held so dear was now ridiculing me as the one who has fallen from grace. Inappropriate or not due to staff and inmate relations, I could only thank this C.O. for his consideration. In his eyes at least, there was still a mutual respect and understanding.

Later that evening, I placed a call to my mother and told her what had occurred. She and my sisters were infuriated, and wanted to call the Warden of the institution and the State Highway Patrol to express their displeasure. Albeit, through tears, I was able to convince them otherwise, and ensured them that I was alright. Though the honest truth was that I was anything but alright. I laid in my bed that night with my Bible firmly grasped, and I meditated upon a scripture. 2 Chronicles 20:15;

> *Be not afraid nor dismayed by reason of this great multitude; for the battle is not yours, but God's.*

I then silently prayed until I drifted off to sleep.

LET GO & LET GOD

As time has haphazardly and aimlessly drifted by, I've come to notice more and more that each phone conversation with my wife becomes that of all she is doing on my behalf reference to my case. She seems to savor in the moment as she discusses my case with me, informing me of all that my attorney is or is not doing. One day after one such tiresome conversation, I came across a scripture during my time of reading which expressed my thoughts towards my situation. 1 Corinthians 2:5;

> *That your faith should not stand in the wisdom of men,*
> *but in the power of God.*

It seems the more I try to remain focused on the Lord and His Word, the more my mind and judgment is clouded with discussions regarding my case. I was told that I needed my attorney. This opinion paved my heart to a passage of scripture. Because in truth, there is only One that I need. Isaiah 48:9-11 reads;

> *For my name's sake will I defer mine anger, and for my*
> *praise will I refrain for thee, that I cut thee not off. Behold,*
> *I have chosen thee in the furnace of affliction. For mine*
> *own sake, even for my own sake, will I do it: for how should*
> *my name be polluted? And I will not give my glory unto*
> *another.*

I cannot waiver. My faith and trust is in the Lord, and in Him alone. So with that, I entertained no further conversation regarding the happenings of my case.

———◆———

As time has passed, it's felt of late that I've been standing on a train track in regards to my marriage. Though I can't see or hear it, I feel the vibration of the train coming underneath my feet. I can't completely identify the origin, yet, the signal light off was rapidly coming into view. I felt the need to prepare myself for the collision which lies ahead.

Later that same night, I talked with the inmate whom I befriended on the day I was given my job assignment. For some unfortunate reason, I felt that I could trust him. He reminded me of a conversation he and I once were engaged in while walking around the institution track. He said to me, *"Luke, as hard as it may be for you to accept it, I believe you know what God is preparing you for, and what He is doing in your life."* He paused before continuing as if to judge my reaction. *"I believe that if you were honest with yourself, then you would also know that He has been revealing it to you for a while now."* He recollected a verse that I once quoted to him, 2 Chronicles 20:15 & 17;

> *Be not afraid nor dismayed by reason of this great multitude; for the battle is not yours, but God's. Ye shall not need to fight in this battle: set yourselves, stand ye still, and see the salvation of the Lord with you.*

He recollected how this verse was presented to me. It wasn't through prayer, or a dream, or any spiritual revelation, but rather from my wife once encouraging me that she felt the Lord had wanted me to read and meditate upon this verse. My friend stated that I probably thought it to be for any other reason than its original source of origin – which was God's preparing me for what's to come. He appeared to be cautious, yet assured, as if it were some other entity speaking through him as he profoundly told me a statement that was spoken to me by my Christian friend at the county jail. As he turned to face me directly he said to me, *"Yes. You did put your wife before God. You are unequally yoked, and God is revealing this and Himself to you now, so that you will understand why and what He is going to do."*

Seemingly, being full of lore, he continued, *"Be honest with yourself Luke. You've been in denial for too long, and it's now time for God to intervene and to set things right in your life. Luke, God is asking you a question; 'Why are you still calling her?' Like that scripture reads, stand still, and watch Him work."* At that moment, it was as though I was suddenly inflicted with lockjaw and could not speak a word. I was left only to walk around the track with these words and thoughts cemented in my mind, as I braced myself once more for the collision yet to come. Though this time, I'm secure with the assurance that I have someone fighting this battle for me. From that moment forward, I stood still.

TRAGIC LOSSES

One evening after the late afternoon count, I ventured to the outside recreation area intent on working out. As I began to go through the routine of exercising for reasons I couldn't grasp, my heart suddenly became clouded and overwhelmed with sadness. Immediately, I thought of home. I walked briskly back to the pod with a sentiment to call someone – anyone in my family. I placed a call to my baby sister, and the tone of her voice spoke volumes. Instantly, with the fear of her response I asked, *"What's wrong?"* Her voice seemed to quiver and became timid, and with apprehension she replied, *"Um, Lukie, I've got some bad news."* My heart became dejected, and my spirit left me as she said, *"Grandma died this morning."* It was with those words that I understood the instant sadness in my heart. As I held the phone in silence, I quickly searched the pod for someone to talk to – something to grasp and hold on to. But there was no one. There was nothing. So I stood empty, clutching the phone in disbelief. Though my sister was silent, I could almost hear each tear drop as they ran down her face onto the receiver. After a few moments of silence with tears of my own streaming down my face, I soberly said to her, *"I'll call you back."* I stood in the crevice of the phone stall trying to stop the profusion of tears that dampened my face. As I turned, there stood my Christian friend shooting a game of pool, and as he looked up and saw me, he immediately placed the pool stick on the table, and nodded his head in a motion for me to follow him outside. We walked around the track, and I wept like a child as I told him about the passing of my grandmother. No words were spoken by him, but they didn't need to be. He was there, and for me that was enough. I once heard a television pastor speak of the passing of his mother. He said of all the people that were there at his home, giving the *"I'm sorry for you loss,"* and the, *"She's in a better place,"* what meant the most to him was a friend who was just there. He sat in a chair next to him and said nothing. But he was there. As we somberly walked around the track, he was there. That meant everything to me at that moment. He walked with me until I couldn't cry anymore, and then with the most genuine concern he asked, *"Are you good bro?"* To which I silently and lightly chuckled and said, *"Yes my friend, I am. Thank you."*

Later that night, as I lay in my bed glaring at the ceiling of my cell, the warmth from my tears filled my cheeks as I cried softly. My mind was absorbed, and deeply fixed with thoughts of concern for my mother. I could only imagine the anguish she must have felt with her mother passing away. It was then to that I realized that grandma was called home one day after her 92nd birthday. When the evening count cleared, I wanted to place a call to my mother to ensure myself of her wellbeing. Upon exiting the cell, I noticed that there were two female officers sitting at the podium of the pod and both of them had their eyes fixated on me. As I rounded the upper tier of the range and walked down the stairs, I observed one of them lean over to the other and whisper as they continued to glare at me. While I stood waiting for a phone to come open, I could sense that I was being talked about by these two officers so purposely. I cast a gaze in their general direction, and caught their eyes meeting up with mine. I so badly wanted to express to them how their constant heedless stairs began to arouse and incense me. Then, right at the height of my frustration, another inmate approached me and said, *"You know those officers are talking about you don't you?"* I said to him, *"Yes, but I'm trying to overlook them!"* He then leaned in close to me and whispered, *"I was standing close to the desk and as you were coming down the stairs they were talking about you being a State Trooper. I think one of them was married to a Trooper."* In an effort to let them know that I knew that I was the topic of their conversation, I took one more glance at them. I then focused my attention on the task at hand which was to contact my mother.

⟫◈⟪

Though she tried with every effort to conceal it, as she answered the phone, I could instantly hear the enormous distress in her voice. Even though she was deeply struggling, she undertook the exertion to calm me by saying, *"Momma just sat up in her favorite chair and simply fell asleep. We went to her apartment to check on her because she didn't answer her phone this morning, and that's how we found her. She was taking a nap in her chair."* She then asked me a question that was very difficult for me to answer. Quite frankly, it was one that I could never be prepared to give an answer to. She asked, *"Lukie, we talked with the Central Office of the prison system. Do you want us to make arrangements for you to see your Grandmother?"* For the sake of my mother, I fought with everything in me, but tears profusely, surged down my face like a stream of gushing water. While I tried to gather myself to respond to her question my mother said to me, *"Momma always prayed that God would perform a miracle for you to come home."* But I didn't want it to be for this reason, so I told my mother, *"I want my memory of grandma to be as it was when I saw her last."* And though her soul and spirit is at rest, subconsciously, I didn't want her memory of her grandson to be in chains and shackles.

The day of my grandmother's funeral my mind was consumed with thoughts of my mother. My heart was marked by such remorse for not being there with her and for her. The excessive blows of life have treated my mother so harshly, as she's had to deal with the anguish of two great losses in her life. The loss of her only son being in prison, and now the loss of her mother. My heart mourns more for her than it does for the loss of my own grandmother. My mother is my heart, and right now that part of me is aching. The Sunday following the funeral services, my family came to visit me. It was a very quiet and somber visit, with everyone still feeling the unremitting grief of grandma's death. Throughout the stint of our visit, silently, without a word being spoken, we mourned our loss.

As the next few weeks have drifted by, the days of my incarceration appear to be more and more difficult to endure. I so desperately long to be home. With the approach of father's day, I ache to be with my children. I aspire to share in their everyday lives with each phone conversation I have with them. In my distress, I sat in the confines of my cell and wept when I received father's day cards from them and the pictures that one of my daughters sent to me. They were pictures of their past when they were very young – pictures of a time that seemed so long ago. My heart melted as I read the words on one of my daughter's cards to me. It read;

> *To a father who has never stopped looking out for his daughter, from a daughter who has never stopped looking up to her Dad.*

When I read these words, I realized that where I am is of no matter because to her I am *still* someone that she looks up to. Through this card, I can hear what they have so often ensured and tried to instill in me, *"That's our daddy, no matter what!" OH!* How I pray for the day to be with them again! I miss them so much!

A few days later, I thought this day was close at hand. One Tuesday afternoon during count time, I heard keys outside of my cell door. The sergeant who is in charge of our pod entered my cell and said, *"McCormick, you have legal mail!"* He showed me where to sign, but spoke no other words to me. As he left my cell, I quickly opened the large envelope containing an abundance of paperwork which I observed as being the appeal my attorney filed on my behalf with the Appellant Court. Instantly, I wondered, *"Is this it God?"* With the paperwork in my hands, I crouched to my knees and lifted it towards heaven and said, *"Lord please bless this appeal, and touch the hearts of those to whom it will be sent. Lord, let this be for Your glory. Dispatch Your angels before the judges, for only You can touch and change the hearts of men."*

Later that evening, I placed a call to my mother and told her about the appeal paperwork I had received. She told me that in turn she was going to call my sisters and other members of the family so that everyone could come together in agreement in prayer.

As the next few weeks elapsed, I was growing increasingly depleted mentally with thoughts of my appeal. Then the day arrived when I was informed by my attorney that oral arguments were scheduled with the Appellant Court. During this time I was working in the commissary, and I could think of nothing else. All throughout the day I stayed in constant silent prayer, pleading for the Lord's favor. At the end of the work day I placed a call home to my mother, and she told me that she couldn't bear to be there, but my sisters and brother-in-law informed her that it all went very well. I was then able to speak with my attorney who confidentially told me that things went well and I just have to await the Judge's decision. The one thing about this incarcerated journey that's become very evident is that waiting can be *extremely* toilsome, especially when it's something that you so desperately desire. For the next few days I prayed fervently for God's favor with the Judges, yet, still, no decision came forth. One night, after many days of laboring in my soul, I stood in the warmth of the shower and prayed earnestly; *"Lord, I need You. My trust and hope lies in You, and You alone. Please dear Lord God, if it be Thy will, grant me Your favor with this appeal, and deliver me from prison. Lord, I want to go home to my family."* It was then while with my eyes closed standing under the water spicket, that I heard these words, *"Trust me."* It was at that moment that I let go. I let go of the questions to which I had no answers and that have been plaguing my mind. I took rest in Him.

———◇◆◇———

With my mind being consumed by so much, the approach of my birthday escaped me. I couldn't help but formulate in my mind how wonderful it would be to be home by the time it arrived. I began receiving cards from my family which truly warmed my heart, but the most satisfying, yet, gut-wrenching were those I received from my children. On one particular afternoon, after coming in from work at the commissary, I had to close myself inside the confines of my cell while reading cards from my daughters. Tears enveloped my eyes as I read the words:

> *While he is many things to different people – a hard worker, a good buddy, or a responsible guy – to me, my dad is my hero. With everything else he has to do, he still makes me feel like I'm just as important as anything else in his world. He listens to me, and cares about the things that matter to me. He encourages me, and makes me feel like I can succeed at everything I do. I'll always look up to this hero of mine, and be grateful that I'm the one who gets to call him dad.*

Before I could recover from these words I read the card from my other daughter.

> *You've always been a great role model. You never tried to act like a big deal, but somehow I always knew you were. And every year you prove a little more how right I was. Happy Birthday Daddy!*

Oh! Lord help me stop these tears! My heart aches with such an elevation of pain! There is no greater solace for a father to have than to know that no matter the circumstance or situation, his kids will always think of him as being their hero and role model. There is no category of words to express or utter how I felt this day.

<hr/>

Later this same night, I laid motionless as sleep abandoned me, and I was consumed with the many thoughts that traversed and enveloped my mind. At one point during the early morning hours, I felt a cool chill brush across my face and I rolled over prostate and gazed out of the cell window. I took notice of a thick haze of fog which encircled and encompassed the perimeter of the fence which stood in the perimeter of my vision. I must have fallen into a temporary slumber at some point during my toil because I awoke to tears streaming down my face. In a comatose state, I sat up directly in the bed, and with an undertone I muttered the words, *"Why did you do that daddy?"* I quickly glanced down at my cell mate to ensure that I hadn't awakened him with my stirring. I would have believed I was dreaming had it not been for the tears which now quilted my face, and the sudden presence of anxiety which apprehended my spirit. I was literally sitting erect in my bed at 4:00 am weeping for reasons that I didn't yet know. It wasn't until later, when I went to my job at the commissary that my early morning exploits came to fruition.

While working at the counter, my boss received a call in his office. He came out and said to me passionately, *"Mr. McCormick, the chaplain wants to see you in his office."* Initially, I thought to have not understood what he said, but the glares of concern of the other inmates working with me left no question that I heard him correctly. My stomach seemed to droop to my feet. My boss unlocked the front door and tapped me on the shoulder as a quiet hush filled the air of the commissary. As I walked toward the building where the chaplain's office was, it felt as though I was walking outside of my body. I felt numbness in my legs, and with each step I took I shuddered. I quivered in fear from not knowing why he would want to see me at this juncture in my incarceration given that I had never spoken to this man personally. Other than greeting him at church services and Bible study, he never spoke a word to me, even with the passing of my grandmother. However, I did understand that usually the only time someone is called to see the chaplain is regarding tidings from home. I prayed this wasn't one of those times. Upon entering the building, I could see down the long hallway and the chaplain standing directly in front of his office as if he was awaiting my arrival. My eyes were fixated on him as I came within closer proximity. Upon approaching his office, he gestured with a nod and said softly, *"Come on in Luke, and close the door."* The gaze that he exhibited was one that I hoped to never see again. I felt a massive sense of restlessness come over me as I sat nervously in a chair facing his desk. With a pensive and melancholy tone, he said with sadness, *"I received a call from your sister this morning. Your father passed away."* Instantly, I slouched in the chair with excruciating pain relentlessly running rapidly through my body! At once, my heart felt as though it was beating out of my chest. Suddenly, I was overridden with guilt for not being there! I wasn't there for my father! The chaplain quietly observed me as I was weeping like a lost child for his father who was not there. My body trembled as I sat slumped over in the chair with my face in my hands, and tears dropping like rain onto the carpet beneath me. I swayed back and forth, while crying for my father and visualizing his face. The chaplain reached in his desk for some tissue and extended his hand to me before asking, *"Would you like to call home?"* Through my tears I responded, *"Yes please,"* and he dialed my mother's phone number. When I heard her voice, I cried all the more! She calmly tried to comfort me as she explained to me all that had occurred. She told me that while my father was hospitalized, due to some unknown complications and ailments, his conditioned worsened through the night. She said that at approximately 4:00 a.m. my father lost consciousness and wasn't breathing. She told me, *"He was gone!"* She said that the doctors were able to revive him before he inevitably succumbed a couple hours later. With a still hush she said to me, *"Lukie, he went on to be with the Lord."* Oh! How I bawled while she told me all of this! I couldn't believe that my daddy was dead! He's gone! He's gone, and I wasn't there to say goodbye! I told my mother about what had happened with me earlier that morning, and with a yell she hollered out, *"Jesus!"* She said to me, *"Luke, maybe in your subconscious you were asking your dad why he came back, why did he let them resuscitate him when he just wanted to go."* She continued with saying, *"Lukie, your daddy was tired. He has been suffering for a long time. It seemed that the more we all prayed and asked God to heal and keep him here, the more your daddy was trying to tell us through his body language that 'It's okay. Please let me go.' He just wanted to go home."* It was then that I realized that my waking in the early morning hour of 4:00 am was precisely the time of my father's reviving. As he was telling my family, I too, was telling him, *"Daddy, it's okay. Go ahead, and let go."* Although I knew daddy was tired of all the tests, the needle probes, and pains which riddled his body, however, selfishly, I wasn't ready to let him go. I didn't want my daddy to be gone. Like my family, I also prayed for the Lord to heal him of all of his aches and pains. He did, in His own way. There is a scripture in Isaiah 55:8 which reads;

> *For my thoughts are not your thoughts, neither are your ways my ways, saith the Lord.*

Just as with my grandmother, my mother asked if I wanted reservations to be made for me to come home and view my father's body. Again, I told her no, because I wanted to remember him just as he was. And even though I knew he was not there, I didn't want for my father to ever again see his son in shackles and chains. I told my mother that I would call her later, and I handed the phone back to the chaplain. He asked me if I would be alright, and then he silently prayed with me before I left his office.

Anguish and guilt engulfed my heart. I got back to the pod and enclosed myself in my cell as I passed other inmates while tears streamed down my face. At one point I looked up and noticed another inmate standing at my cell door watching me. He must have talked with the C.O. working the pod regarding my circumstance because knowing how news travels rapidly across the grounds of this institution, my cell door suddenly popped open. He quietly entered, and stood leaning on my sink. He didn't utter a word. I again thought about the story that pastor spoke about regarding the death of his mother. The one friend who was just there and not saying a word. Seemingly, with his arms crossed as if he was standing guard, he silently just stood and watched. I wept. With my head crouched and tears covering the floor of my cell, I cried till it seemed I had nothing left. As my cell mate entered, the two of them stepped out onto the upper range giving me time to gather myself. I then walked out and thanked the other inmate, and he said, *"I'm here if you need anything."*

I called home each day and cried profusely to my mother and sister. As the day drew near for the funeral, the pain and anguish was too overwhelming for me, and I couldn't bear it. I wept bitterly. I placed my feelings in words as I wrote a personal letter to my father, and I expressed to him how I felt as his son. I placed a call to my two daughters, and asked if they would represent me by reading this letter at the funeral services. Until I'm able to say it myself when I'm home visiting his burial site, this was my personal goodbye to my father, and I wanted my daughters to share in it with me.

I spent the morning of the funeral services confined in my cell. I had earlier asked my supervisor if it would be okay for me to leave early to which he told me, *"Of course. Mr. McCormick you take all the time you need."* I knew the services were scheduled to begin at 11:00 am, and my eyes stayed fixated on the clock. Each passing second was filled with thoughts, images, and reflections of times spent with my father. I thought about times and conversations that he and I shared here in the visiting room. Late Sunday mornings, and early afternoons were our time as father and son. We spoke about things that no one else in my family knew about, like the accident concerning my son which ultimately led to my demise and my incarceration. He knew about the feelings I had concealed concerning my son and that I never shared with anyone. One Sunday morning during a visit he said to me, *"Luke, I know how you felt when your son had the accident and lost his eye. I know the reason that you never talked about it with anyone is because you blamed yourself. You thought if you would have been there it never would have happened."* As tears streamed down my face, he continued with words that only a father could give to a son. *"Son, it was not your fault. You have to let it go and forgive yourself, because you weren't there for a reason. All of this time you've been carrying this on your shoulders, and it's time to let it go son."* It was at that moment that I did. With the loving and caring words of my father, I relinquished the burden of my son's accident and surrendered it into the hands of God. So now, as I sat in the corner of my cell, watching the hands of the clock methodically approaching 11:00 a.m. I thought of times spent with my dad. I thought about how a single event in one's life can change life forever. The reflection of this one visit with my father changed the course of my life, and it's one that I'll never forget. I'd give anything for just one more visit – just one more talk. I'd give anything for just one more time to embrace my father. My daddy's gone, and no hurt and pain that I feel can bring him back.

So for now, I'm grateful for the images of reflection of times spent and shared. I'm grateful for the life of my father.

⟫•◇•⟪

The weekend following the death and burial of my father I was visited by members of my family. It seemed to be everyone's endeavor to comfort me as they conveyed how beautiful the *going home* service was for my father. We shed no tears, only laughter, yet, my spirit churned, and I felt something amiss among us in the atmosphere. The following Sunday, I was revisited by my mother, one of my sisters, and brother-in-law. It was then that I learned what was so troubling to my spirit.

The three of them gawked at each other as if they were trying to decide who was going to tell me the bad news that I felt was coming. Eventually, with sorrowful afflicted eyes, my brother-in-law said somberly, *"Your appeal was denied."* Instantly, dazed and dumbfounded, with many questions racing through my mind I asked, *"Did my attorney call?"* My eyes bounced back and forth between the three of them as my heart searched for answers. My brother-in-law softly replied, *"No. Two days ago, it was briefly announced on the local news that 'State Trooper McCormick's appeal has been denied by the Appellant Court'."* I was exasperated, and whatever ounce of strength I had left in me was depleted! Right there, in the midst of the visiting room amongst other inmates and their families, I wept bitterly. I began pounding on the table that divided my family and me saying, *"I don't understand! God help me! I just don't understand!"* I glanced up at my mother, and tears were streaming down her face. I became very angry at God and I said to Him, *"I've done all that You've asked of me! I continually seek Your face, and stay in Your word! God, I don't understand! I don't know what it is that you want me to do!"* It was at that point that I realized I've been broken. All of my strength; all of my might; every ounce and fiber of my being was broken! I had no fight left in me. I suddenly felt the loving touch of my mother rubbing my arm, which caused me to weep even more, because I felt somehow that I had let her down. I wanted this for her more so than for myself, so that she wouldn't have to suffer any longer. My sister sat silently, but I sensed that her eyes never left me. I felt her concern and anguish for her brother. To make matters worse, my brother-in-law said to me, *"Luke, I'm sorry man, but we have to get back to Michigan. We only came back today to tell you this because we thought that you should know."* I then saw as my brother-in-law briefly spoke with one of the C.O.s' working in the visiting room. I later learned that due to my uncharacteristic actions, they were concerned as well and wanted to have the chaplain present. However, they later declined, and decided to just keep a watchful eye on me. With that, I stood and embraced my mother as I tried to clear my face of the tears that vigorously streamed down my face. I was left alone standing in the mist of obscurity that shrouded and overclouded my heart. I felt on the verge of a nervous breakdown. I know the Bible speaks of Him not putting more on you than you can bear. However, this is a grief, coupled with the recent losses of my father and grandmother that are too immense for me to endure.

I spent the next several days trying to understand what happened. I spent a lot of time laying prostate on my cell floor during count time crying profusely. In my futile search for answers, I was finally able to contact my attorney, and by this time I was enraged! I simply and frankly asked him, *"What happened? I thought you told me that if you had to write a script it couldn't have gone any better?"* His answer infuriated me even further as with a lack of concern he replied, *"I did think that, but I don't know what happened. I don't know what to tell you."* Words left me, but if I could have gotten my hands on him at that point, I'd be incarcerated for other circumstances! Again, I felt alone. Unexpectedly, the conversation my father and I had concerning my son's accident came back to my thought process. It was as though God was reminding me of how I never once came to Him, but kept it all within. I was in a broken state, and suddenly I found myself crying, and praying fervently and earnestly to God, telling Him all that was on my heart! I was angry and mad with God because truly I believed that I was in the midst of coming home. It was through this brokenness and openness that I began to feel a transformation beginning to take place within me.

Because of the judgment that went against me from the Appeals Court, I was simultaneously humiliated and humbled.

It took a while for me to recover from the great losses that I had endured. I didn't want to read my Bible, I didn't want to talk to God, nor attend any Bible study sessions, or church services. Then one day, I was compelled to read Jeremiah 20:7, 9:

> *O Lord, thou hast deceived me, and I was deceived: thou art stronger than I, and hast prevailed: I am in derision daily, every one mocketh me. Then I said, I will not make mention of him, nor speak any more in his name. But his word was in mine heart as a burning fire shut up in my bones, and I was weary with forbearing, and I could not stay.*

It was then that I had realized just how displeased I was with the Lord in not granting my appeal, and also with the death of my father. But just like the prophet Jeremiah in this verse of scripture, His word was rooted deep within me, and I couldn't stay this way. So eventually, I dusted myself off from all of the despair that loomed so heavily over me, and I did as King David when all was against him in the book of 1 Samuel 30:6, *I encouraged myself in the Lord.*

PAYING IT FORWARD

As the next few months cascaded by, the Christmas season rapidly approached. I've always loved this time of year, because I bask in all of the festivities and wonder the season bestows. Though I've missed being home for the past two Christmases, I sensed however that this one would be even more excruciating, with all that my family has had to endure over this past year. One early afternoon, a few days prior to Christmas, I was feeling lowly and yearning to be with my family. I placed a call to my mother, and I could hear the same heartache through the inflection of her voice. She wanted me home just as much as I desired to be there. The loss of her mother, my father, and her son, once again not being home for Christmas, I believe was too much for her to bear! As we talked, I could hear the spoon strike the side of her cup as she stirred her coffee. I began to picture her sitting there in her kitchen gazing out of the window as she slowly sipped her coffee. I imagined the memory of me sitting there with her as I used to do for the stint of time I lived with her. *OH!* What I wouldn't do to be there with her now, sharing in a loving conversation between mother and son.

As Christmas morning arrived, I again called my mother's home knowing that all of my family would be gathered there for our annual Christmas brunch. While talking with a friend of the family, I could hear the joy and laughter ring out and resonate through the phone. I asked to speak with my mother, and it seemed that the same aching heart from a few days ago still lingered on. Suddenly, and unexpectedly, the family friend's voice returned. I asked her, *"What happened to my mother?"* Before she could respond to my question, I heard my mother's soft cries in the background. With tears now beginning to whelp in my eyes my friend said, *"Your mom is a little emotional right now Lukie, but she's alright."* I choked back tears while I spoke to my children and a few other family members, and was comforted when once again I heard my mother's laughter. God forbid that I had to spend another Christmas in prison; I vowed that I would never again call home on that day. I would never place this burden on my mother or myself again. This was a grief that was too much for either of us to bear.

With the coming in of the New Year, I began preparing myself for a change of venue concerning my job. I learned from the unit manager that I was selected to be a tutor in the education department. Tutors work in the school helping inmates obtain a GED. I attended a class given by the institution, and upon completion I received certification as a certified tutor. To know that I was hand selected by the institution and education staff restored in me a sense of honor. For the first time in a long time, I felt good about myself because I knew that I was going to be able to help others. For an instant, it kind of made me reflect back on my days as a State Trooper. I know there is no true comparison between the two entities, however, this certification and selection gives me a sense of self-worth. Though I enjoyed my time and the people at the commissary, with all that I've undergone in my time of incarceration, this is a much embraced change. During this same time I was also selected to participate in a mentor program called J.O.P., (Juvenile Offender program). I was informed by the director of this program that due to my background that I was the perfect candidate. This program centers on troubled teenagers and their parents within the juvenile court system. They are recommended and sent by judges and prosecutors to come through the prison system to be mentored and counseled by chosen inmates.

The following Thursday evening the program was to begin. Myself and several other inmates stood in a type of gauntlet as the juveniles were brought into the institution and formed a line between us. Suddenly, some of the inmates began yelling and screaming and getting in the faces of these young men. It appeared to me to be more of a *scared straight* program than that of mentoring. I stood back and observed as these inmates appeared to take this opportunity to unleash some of their pinned up frustrations on these juveniles. As soon as the thought that *"I didn't sign up for this,"* came to mind, myself and a few other inmates were called to the institution visiting room. Upon entering, I observed that the room was occupied with the parents of these young men, and we were told to sit in chairs which faced them. My eyes quickly scanned their faces, most of which were mothers, and they were immersed in trepidation. The room was full of stillness as each inmate and parent seemed to form a judgment upon each other. The director then stood and said, *"This portion of the program is called the meet and greet session."* He directed his attention towards the parents and said, *"Each inmate will now stand and give his name, his number, his crime, and his time."* With that, one by one we stood and conveyed this information. *"Aggravated murder; murder; felonious assault; rape; aggravated burglary."* Although, I viewed this as something to buffer or neutralize the fear for these parents, however, the trepidation seemed to increase with each crime mentioned. In turn, one by one the parents then described in detail the circumstance for their son's presence in this program. I then was able to speak candidly and personally with the parent of the son I would be counseling. As she spoke, the pain and anguish this mother felt about her son left me only to think of my mother speaking about me. With each word she spoke, her eyes were fixated on mine. I could sense the question drifting in her mind, *"What's your story?"* As she finished telling me about her son, I felt it only right to quench the careening question that her mind held. I looked at her plainly and said pungently, *"My situation here is unique compared to some others. I used to be a State Trooper."* Her reaction startled me. She gazed at me with the most heartfelt glance, and as tears formed like whelps in her eyes, she asked sheepishly, *"You used to be a State Trooper?"* The way that she directed that question to me caused me to withstand tears of my own that I felt forming. I shared with her brief portions of my story, and it seemed that we formed a bond of understanding. Although, for her, at that moment, it seemed it was no longer just about her son, but the compassion she now displayed for me.

For the next three weeks, I was able to counsel and mentor her son, sharing with him the framework of life's choices from both sides of the criminal justice system. On the last day of the program, I was able to have a one on one session with both the juvenile and his mother. My mind was consumed with thoughts of my own mother having to come into this very room to visit her son. I looked him directly in the eye and I tried inspiring to capture his attention. I said to him harshly, *"Look at your mother! Look at this woman sitting next to you! You come into a place like this and this will be the only friend you have! All of those so called friends that you think that you have now will become extinct."* He dropped his head and I noticed tears dropping on the floor beneath him. I then calmly told him, *"Due to wrong choices I made in my life, I've caused my mother to have to walk through those doors. I did that to her. Those same tears you see in your mother's eyes are tears I'm forced to ingest every week. Because of me, my mother endures this incarceration. She is the other side of the sentence. You have a chance to prevent your mother from being like mine is. It's up to you."*

As this program ended with this particular juvenile, there were others following just like him. There were other mothers suffering just as his was. But with each session, I gained more perspective about the art the helping others. I took away from them as much as I gave.

PAST REFLECTIONS

It's been about 8 months since I broke off all communication with my wife. During this time, I've had the opportunity to have my eyes opened in so many areas regarding our marital relationship. I began to reflect on times and events after the incident when my wife would endeavor to instill in others how we had a wonderful marriage and how our marriage was of God. However, it seemed as though her attempts were futile, and ineffective to others. I believe that all could see that our marriage was based on anything other than what she portrayed. I recall a conversation my sister had with my wife and me one night during the time that we were staying in her home. She sat us down and told us, *"However hurtful, I would be amiss not to tell you that the Holy Spirit wants me to give this scripture to you. I hope that the two of you can receive it."* The scripture was taken from Matthew 12:25, and as we took the Bible, and my wife read it first, she became infuriated! The scripture read;

A house divided against itself, cannot stand.

As I reflect on this verse of scripture, I'm reminded of the walk on the track with my friend, when he asked, *"Why are you still calling her?"* In looking back, I understand that this was a battle far greater than I was prepared to fight. There were forces which occupied my marriage that I didn't know of. However hurtful, I believe that God was revealing to me that which my heart always knew. Instinctively, with the expiration of each passing day, I was being shown simply what God was preparing me for. Although God had given me such a peace about it that I was able to constrain the urges, but there were times when I was tempted to contact my wife. There were times when I feared that my lack of contact really hurt her. But my fear of the Lord overrode these anxieties. Suddenly, during this time when I stood firm, I began to receive letters from my wife. They weren't letters of concern about why I stopped contacting her, but rather, I felt they were words to lure me into responding. Through communication with my family, and directives of those who know her, I became more and more cognizant of this woman that I married. Yet, beyond this, one day I received a message through a television evangelist. As she was coming to the close of her segment she said abruptly, *"God will not let me end this until I give a message to somebody out there. I don't know who this is for, but the Holy Spirit said for you to read Exodus 14:14."* And with that, she closed her segment. My eye ducts filled with tears and I grasped my Bible, while reading this verse of scripture.

The Lord shall fight for you, and ye shall hold your peace.

There is an old Christian adage that cites, *"God said it, I believe it, and that settles it!"* Although, the true meaning of this adage is God said it, and *that* settles it! So with that and in that I stood still. I trusted God.

In recent nights my mind began to drift. I found myself recalling memories and times about being a State Trooper. I thought about old acquaintances and the different patrol posts which I had worked. I wondered what these acquaintances had thought about me, and think of me now since my crime. I reflected on a time when I was held in such high admiration only to have my image tarnished by one self-assertive act. I lay prostrate in my bed one night, and thought of the day that I received a phone call while at my mother's home. My district commander had wanted to meet with me in the parking lot of the Highway Patrol Post to which I spent the larger part of my career. It was there, on that day, that I was given a letter of termination signed by the Lieutenant Governor of the State of Ohio. At the time of my termination, no charges had been filed against me. My only crime at that time was the embarrassment to the organization of the State Highway Patrol. I had become a blemish to their image, and I had to go. *Uh!* I repulse and sicken myself! I seemingly had it all; the respect, the accolades, and the accomplishments of a 9 ½ year career were all disrobed with the words, *"You are hereby terminated from the Department of Public Safety. Namely, the Ohio State Highway Patrol."* Just as with this night, I left behind the confines of these prison walls with memories of a time in my life that's departed me.

The following morning, I awoke and turned on my cell mate's radio. A local Christian station began to play the most tranquil melodies, and the words struck a harmonious chord which soothed my spirit. I sat in the cell alone and found solace in eluding the remembrances of times gone by.

Later that day, as if they discerned my affliction, I received Valentine's Day greeting cards from my children. As I sat enclosed in my cell, I read one of the cards from my daughter.

> *To my father, my very first valentine. I hope you don't mind if I congratulate myself on my very good fortune for being born to a man like you. A man who is patient, wise, and kind. A man whose endless reassurance and encouragement has made all the difference in my life. You were my very first valentine, and you'll always be at the top of my list.*

As tears streamed down my face, I read the card from my other daughter.

> *I just want you to know that you've always been my hero. And although we are not together, you are always in my heart. I know we will be back together soon. But until then, you keep praying and so will I. But no matter what,*

I will make you proud in all that I do. Happy Valentine's Day daddy, I love you!

My son's card spoke of me being;

The best dad ever! Even though you don't think that we think that of you, we do!

My children's love, devotion, and support far supersede any anguish I've endured with thoughts of the Highway Patrol. Their love is all that I need in life.

FLEECING GOD

After working for only 10 months as a tutor, the teacher that I was working for took a temporary leave of absence. During intersession for the Christmas break, she never returned. She cited stress as her reason for leave. Therefore, I was left jobless, and was resigned to reporting to the school administrator each morning, and helping out where I was needed. Consequently, upon reporting one day, I was approached by the institution chaplain who inquired about working for him. So, while waiting on my teacher's return, I became the chaplain's assistant. During this time, we became very close and had daily discussions and counseling sessions regarding my life. He became not only a close confidant, but a mentor as well. So much so that I was often teased by other inmates and given the title of *baby chap!* The more time he and I spent working together the more intimate our conversations became. There were times that I learned just as much from simply watching his day to day actions as I did from our discussions. I believe that it was God given that my teacher departed as she did because upon her return she and the chaplain came to an agreement that I could balance both duties. It seemed that neither of them wanted to relinquish my services.

One afternoon while working in the chapel, another inmate came to me and asked, *"Did you see your name on the list to see the parole board?"* I chuckled, and told him to stop kidding around when he said, *"No man, I'm serious! On the paper posted in the pod it reads # 429-490 Luther T. McCormick with the word special beside your information."* Unexpectedly, one by one other guys came to the chapel informing me of the same information. I suddenly became overwhelmed and attempted to conceal my face because I could feel tears beginning to whelp in my eyes. The chaplain when he became abreast of this called me into his office, and silently we rejoiced in the Lord's goodness and began to pray. When I later arrived at the pod, I was barraged by inmates who seemed to want to be the first to indulge me about being on this list. I was even approached by the unit manager who said, *"In all the years that I've worked in the prison system, I've never heard of nor seen a guy have a special hearing with the parole board."* I knew that my attorney had filed for executive clemency with the Governor's office; however, I merely held my peace and trusted in the Lord. Later that evening, I placed a call to my mother and informed her that I had a hearing scheduled with the parole board. Instantly, her spirit became revived and exhilarated. She told me that she was going to contact my sisters and other members of the family, and that we all were going to unite in prayer.

My hearing date drew close at hand, and with each passing day, I pondered as to what questions the parole board would ask and what answers I would give. I knew that I held a secret that no one else was privy to, other than God. I remember walking the track of the institution rehearsing over and over again in my mind possible questions that could be asked as my gut churned in fear. Then, one early Sunday afternoon while walking the track, I was suddenly overcome with an overwhelming urge to tell my sister the truth about my convictions. This particular sister to whom I had this sudden urge to confess resides in Michigan. As I slowly cascaded around the track, silently, I told the Lord this; *"Lord, If this is what you want me to do - to confess the events of what truly happened that night, then allow my sister from Michigan to visit me today."* However clever I thought to be, I knew this to be virtually impossible given the fact that visitation would be over before she could have time to arrive, but God had another plan. As I've heard it told many times, He also has a sense of humor. My cunningness was already perceived because no sooner than the words left my thoughts and mouth, my cell mate exited the pod and yelled to me, *"Luke, you have a visit!"* Instantly, the entrails of my stomach penetrated my throat and rendered me breathless. I was traumatized, and jolted, and with each step I traipsed in the direction of the visiting room my legs trembled under me. Yet, even still, I thought it impossible for it to be that sister, but figured it to be anyone but her. Nonetheless, upon entering the visiting room, there she sat smiling, and peering directly in my eyes. At once, my heart sunk for I knew what had to be done. I was enlightened this day on the divine nature and power of the Creator of the universe.

I embraced my sister and brother-in -law and I know they felt the quivering in my body. I felt to be on a mission, so without delay or hesitation I said to her, *"I have something that I have to tell you."* My memory recollected that only a few days prior this same sister, through my mother, gave me the scripture Psalm 24. Verses three and four reads;

> *Who shall ascend into the hill of the Lord? And who shall stand in his holy place? He that hath clean hands, and a pure heart; who hath not lift up his soul unto vanity, nor sworn deceitfully.*

I now knew the path that lies before me. Only, how do you tell someone who has stood by you, loved you, and supported you through the trials and tribulations of your life that you have deceived them. However, as it reads in 1 Samuel 15:22;

> *Behold, to obey is better than sacrifice.*

The communication in my sister's eyes told me that she knew beforehand what I was going to say. Yet, there was no escaping this, and the words had to be spoken. With the silhouette of tears forming in my eyes I woefully said, *"What happened that night was not an accident."* With a loving grin, and as if waiting for so long to hear my confession, my sister calmly said, *"Everyone already knew that Lukie."* I asked, *"Even momma?"* To which she answered, *"Yes. Even momma. We actually talked about it soon after it happened, but we never talked about it with you."* Soon after confessing the events of that fateful night, I felt almost ready to collapse with the mitigation of the stress that overcame me. With a smile beaming across his face and with a sense of relief, my brother-in-law said to me, *"You're going to be alright man!"*

As my hearing date with the parole board inched closer thoughts never ceased as to how I would respond to their questions. One afternoon during count time, I sat on the edge of my bunk reading my Bible when a scripture abruptly came to mind. Luke12:11;

> *When they bring you into the synagogues, and unto magistrates, and powers, take ye no thought how or what thing ye shall answer, or what ye shall say: For the Holy Ghost shall teach you in the same hour what ye ought to say.*

Additionally, during this same time the words of a friend that had written to me came to mind. *"Luke, please don't take this out of God's hands."* With all that traversed in my mind, at that moment, I turned it all over to God and trusted Him.

The day for my hearing arrived. With my wrists being shackled, I sat before the parole board which consisted of two women. I noticed that my case file was opened in front of one of the women, and as she began to introduce herself, in walked a man who I learned was the chairman of the parole board. He told me that he rarely ever sits on panels, but wanted to ensure that he was here for my hearing. After the detailed steps were explained regarding the clemency process, right away the barrage of questions began. I was asked by the woman who had my file before her, *"It says here that three separate prosecutors refused to file charges against you, is that correct?"* I replied, *"Yes ma'am."* She then asked, *"Weren't you once selected as State Trooper of the year by your patrol post, and later awarded as Peace Officer of the year?"* Chagrined, I again responded with, *"Yes ma'am."* The three of them glanced at each other in wonderment while the whole atmosphere in the room changed with my response to one question. As she told me to tell her in my own words what happened that night, it was as though God Himself interrupted my mutterings. She abruptly asked, *"Mr. McCormick, was this an accident?"* With unforeseen tears beginning to stream down my face, and without thought or hesitation, I responded, *"No!"* Again, they glared at each other, and I began to weep profusely and utterly express the regret of my actions that culminated in the events of that night. I confessed everything that led to my wrongdoing and the details of my crime. I recounted how it all began with the tragic event concerning my son.

I realized too that without the talks with my father concerning my son, I couldn't have confessed all that I did this day. Even though he was gone, yet, his presence seemingly was with me, and that gave me strength and reassurance in the time of most significance. The other lady who sat on the panel reached inside of her purse and extended her hand to give me some tissue. Oddly, at that moment, the board members seemed to be as proud of me for coming forth with the truth and accepting full responsibility as I was with the alleviation of this immense wearisome burden. As I flushed the stream of tears from my eyes, the lady who asked the questions gave me an appeasing smile and said, *"Take all the time you need."*

I left the parole member's presence that day with a softening and lightening of spirit. I felt the freedom described in Isaiah 9:4:

> *For thou hast broken the yoke of his burden, and the staff*
> *of his shoulder, the rod of his oppressor.*

I left there knowing that this lie would never again vex or oppress me. This day, I found rest for my soul.

⟫◆⟪

It seems that I had barely made it back to the pod before the news rapidly spread across the compound with my coming forth with the truth. Several inmates revered my decision, however, there were many that secretly derided and ridiculed my judgment. I recall one inmate privately telling me, *"There is no way that I could have done what you did! I would have waited until I got out, if ever, before I would have told the truth. You should have stuck with your story, because I think you messed up your chance of going home by telling the truth!"* I was even told about one of my sisters who said, *"Lukie didn't have to tell the parole board what happened, he had already confessed it to God!"* Although my mother quickly came to my defense by saying, *"What kind of a Christian would he profess to be, if he knows that he's living a lie? God can't bless a mess!"* This same sister when during a visit informed me directly, *"I wouldn't have told them!"* It amazed me that everything seemed fine while I had everyone deceived. Yet, they abhorred the taste of the truth.

One day while working in the chapel, I was approached by the second shift officer who also learned about my acknowledgment to the parole board. As he sat at his desk, he looked squarely in my eyes and said, *"I hope you don't mind, but I've used your testimony on several occasions in church as a testament to what we as Christians are to do in the face of adversity. It took a lot of courage to go against all that the world says you should do, yet, still do the right thing. I'm proud of you, and better still, so is God." You are a walking testimony for so many in here, both staff and inmates."*

A few days after my hearing with the parole board, I was told by the pod officer that the unit's case manager wanted to see me. Upon my arrival to her office, I was advised that she had received a call from my attorney. That same afternoon, I placed a call to my attorney from the chaplain's office. He informed me about a hearing scheduled with the parole board that members of my family could attend. The discourse of our oral exchange startled him, and left him aghast as I advised him, *"I told them the truth about what happened that night. I couldn't bear it any longer."* He seemed perturbed and incensed, yet, attempted to remain composed. As again, I told him, *"I could not continue looking my mother in the eye knowing that I was living a lie. I had to do it! I just had to."* It seemed to me he thought his professional image was now tarnished, and I never heard from him again. All other dealings were represented by his father, who was the patriarch of the firm. My lie has cost me dearly. During this time of my confession, I lost what appears to be the irreclaimable friendship and acquaintance of two fellow law enforcement colleagues who, unbeknownst to them, supported my lie. Many lives were touched and changed due to my deceitfulness, surprisingly, even that of my attorney. For that, and the duress of not being able to bare it any longer, I was compelled to reveal the truth. My confession was a hurdle that I had to conquer, no matter the cost. Through it, I've learned that the ultimate measure of a man is not what he achieves, but rather, it's what he overcomes. This contention was personal and deeply entrenched, and I exult in this triumph.

I spent the morning of the hearing looming on the prospect of being home. I sat in the chapel immersed in deep thought about walking in my mother's back yard barefoot, feeling blades of grass between my toes. I thought about looking toward the sky with my eyes closed and feeling the gentle breeze of freedom brush across my face. *Um*, I thought of home. Just as these thoughts began to overwhelm and consume me, the chaplain entered, and seemed to know my mental state. He asked me to come into his office. He asked me directly, *"Luke, do you ever look back on your life and wonder how all of this happened? Do you ask yourself how did I get here? Do you ever wish that God would have done it all differently?"* This appearing to be a rhetorical question he continued, *"Of course you do."* He then made the most profound statement that seemed to summarize my incarceration. *"How do you stop a runaway train? You derail it! Luke, other than the time you've lost with your family and kids you are all the better after going through this."*

Later that evening, I spoke with my mother and she told me about the hearing. She said that I had a large show of support through family members and friends, some of which spoke on my behalf. The chairman ended the hearing by informing everyone that their recommendation would be forwarded to the Governor for his final decision.

A couple of weeks removed while awaiting the outcome, the chaplain asked me to take a walk with him. Dismal and dispirited, he said, *"It doesn't look good."* Though I knew what he was telling me, I asked unassuming, *"What doesn't look good Chap?"* Before he responded, instantly, I was induced with tears of intense anger and hurt! He said gently, *"I spoke with a member of the parole board, and was informed that your chances for clemency don't look good. You need to prepare yourself."* It was a few days later that I was called to the library by a friend of mine who worked there, and he handed me the local newspaper from my home area. In bold print read the lines;

Ohio State Trooper McCormick's bid for executive clemency denied by The Ohio Parole Board and the State Governor.

Instantly, I began to question my coming forth with the truth and wondered if I had done the right thing. Was everyone that ridiculed me correct by saying that I ruined my own chances for going home? My mother, the chaplain, and all who were involved to witness the hearing believe that this was an act of God in revealing to her what I had always known, that this marriage was not of Him. Yet, that didn't alleviate the pain and churning inside of my gut, and I questioned my decision. The impact of my decision struck the place where I'm most vulnerable when I received a letter from one of my daughters. She simply said, *"Daddy, I just knew that I would be with you soon! This decision hit harder than in the very beginning!"* I often have thoughts of playing with my daughters, and my son running into my arms. But all seemed dashed with the decision that I chose to make that day. My heart wrenched as I felt that once again I let my children down! Just as I felt myself begin to slither into a state of depression, I was placed in a circle one night during Bible study and surrounded by other inmates. One of them began to pray aloud, *"Lord, show Luke the reflection of what he did as an example for others. In going against all odds and confessing his faults before everyone is a witness and testament of how we are to live our lives. Open his eyes Lord, and let him see himself as you see him."* A substance of tears doused the floor beneath me, and I wept bitterly. Later that same night I had a dream. I was sitting with my three children surrounding me, and my younger daughter said, *"Daddy, don't you know that you did the right thing, and that God is going to work it all out!"* Again, I awoke and wept. The following day I received a card from my brother-in-law as further evidence to my amendment. He wrote, *"It takes a lot for us to see ourselves as God sees us, and also to confess it. I'm proud of you brother for what you did."* Through adversity, I'm being taught more and more the degree of love gratuitously bestowed by my family. My mother was deeply concerned about how my loving cousin would feel regarding my confession, and felt the need for me to contact her.

Even she embraced me. I received a card from her that read:

> *When it's easier to stay down, some men choose to get up. When it's easier to be weak, some men choose to be strong. When it's easier to be afraid, some men choose to act courageously. When it's easier to remain deceived, some men choose to know the truth. When it's easier to flee, some men choose to stay. Honor, Integrity, and Wisdom, don't come by easy choices. Take pride today, your choices are celebrated!*

When I read the words on this card it led me to pray and ask the Lord continually, *"Don't let me look like where I came from. You pulled me out of it; the lies and deceptions that encompassed my life. Now Lord, pull it out of me. For this I vow to never have my integrity questioned again."* However, the most compelling words of all came from a letter that I received from my wife, simply telling me to stand on the word of God, and she knows that we must now take separate paths.

With this, I rested. It was several days later when during Bible study the chaplain said, *"The two greatest decisions a man will ever make is whom he will choose to be his God, and whom he will chose to be his wife."* Within the passing of a month, the pod sergeant informed me that I had legal mail to sign for. I received divorce papers filed by my wife. I was left only to consider the verse in Romans 11:33:

> *O the depth of the riches both of the wisdom and knowledge of God! How unsearchable are his judgments, and his ways past finding out!*

The chaplain sat with me in his office and we discussed the issue of my receiving divorce paperwork from my wife. He leaned forward and placed his hands on his desk, and while glaring directly into my eyes he said, *"Luke, you've given enough – you've asked for forgiveness enough; you have paid the ultimate price, and are still. Luke, it's time for you to do as King David did when he lost his son. It's time for you to dust yourself off and go on."* He then read a scripture to me.

Jeremiah 31:18, 19:

> *Thou hast chastised me, and I was chastised, as a bullock unaccustomed to the yoke: turn thou me, and I shall be turned; for thou art the Lord my God. Surely after that I was turned, I repented; and after that I was instructed, I smote upon my thigh: I was ashamed, yea, even confounded, because I did bear the reproach of my youth.*

He continued, *"Luke, you've repented more for the reason of you being here than any person I've ever counseled. It's time to let it go."* With that, while in his presence, I signed the divorce papers and sent them back to the Domestic Relations Court. I let go!

BROKEN ABSENCE — A FATHER'S ANGUISH

The time has come for my oldest daughter's graduation from high school. Even though she knew that I'd be incapable to attend, she still sent me an invitation. I believe that she didn't want me to feel left out any more than I already do. The heartbreak overwhelmed me, and I was submerged in a depth of utter despair. The thought of not seeing her walk across that platform, and she not seeing her father beam with pride as she receives her diploma, tares at the fiber of my soul. I deplore my being here! I placed a call to my daughter and passionately exclaimed my sorrow for not being there for her on her special day. With the softest and sweetest voice she said, *"Don't worry about it Daddy, it's not like it's your fault. I know that if you could be here, you would be on center stage. Please don't feel bad or sorry. It's okay."* At that moment I was struck with a stark reality. My little girl was growing up. Through the wholesome sound in her voice, I couldn't recall a time when I've been more proud.

Later that night I lay restless with my mind on my children and home. I gazed out of my cell window and glared at the lights that reflected from the adjacent pod. My mind traversed, and I wondered how this institution looks at night from the roadway as vehicles pass by. I wonder, *"How does it look just beyond the fence on the other side of freedom? Can they see me looking out through the bars of my window? Can they see me longing to be where they are?"* As I lay prostate, exasperated and drowning with my thoughts, I began to reminisce. I thought about the times when I was a State Trooper. How I would come home during lunch break and my son would always run to the driver's side of my patrol car, jump up and hang onto the door. He would scream with excitement, *"Turn the lights on Daddy!"* I'd chuckle with his joy as I'd watch my daughters playing tether ball in the yard with their little girlfriends. I reflected on a day during the time of my trial. After spending a late afternoon with me, I was dropping my son off at his mother's home. I was greeted in the driveway by my niece who, in extreme anxiety, and with tears streaming down her face said to me, *"Uncle Lukie, you need to come in and talk to your daughter."* As I exited the car in trepidation I asked, *"What's wrong?"* She silently guided me into the house, and there sat my younger daughter and my children's mother with tear stained faces. I asked, *"Where is she?"* With no response, my eyes shifted like a gaze of radar to the front room portion of the house where my oldest daughter stood. I approached, and with her arms clasped across her chest her heavy heart gloomed, and shown through her eyes. Tears streamed profusely down her face and immediately I was overridden with guilt. Gently, I placed my arm around her and asked, *"What's wrong sweetheart?"* Her response pierced my heart like a sharp knife. *"I'm scared Daddy! What are they going to do to you?"* Instantly, I became aware of the impact that this trial had on her. She stood crying her little heart out for the fear of what was to become of her father. With my arm around her, I guided her to the steps of the front porch. There we sat and held one another. A father and his daughter crying in each other's arms. Other than the injured effect of my son's accident, I haven't felt so depleted. I lay drowning this night in the pool of resentment. Not only for the wrong choices I made in my life, but more for how those choices has affected the lives of my children. This night I reflected, and I remember.

The day swiftly approached for another birthday to be spent while incarcerated. I so deeply desired to see my children. My eyes haven't beheld them since the days preceding my trial. Oh how intensely I've missed them! Thoughts of holding them and immersing myself in them never escape my mind. I glanced out of the window which faced the entry way of the institution and observed as inmates families gathered. No sooner than the anticipation of these thoughts came to mind about my children that my focus careened to a little boy and young girl who gallivanted across the parking lot. With an eruption of exuberance I blared, *"My babies! That's my babies!"* Instantly, I became anxious and jittery, and bounced around the window like a dog when it rides in a car! Oblivious of my surroundings, I mouthed aloud, *"My kids are here! My kids came to see me for my birthday!"* Tears filled my eyes, and I went to my cell to pull myself together before the C.O. would call me for my visit. When I came through the door of the visiting room, my eyes instantly gravitated to where they were sitting. After checking in at the officer's desk, I approached them, and I noticed too that their eyes were fixated on me. My younger daughter instantaneously stood and embraced me. *OH!* She felt so good in my arms! She whispered, *"Now I can see for myself that you're okay."* I gulped back tears, and one by one I cradled them in my arms. I greeted their mother also who had accompanied them. Wordless, I articulated my appreciation for her bringing them with a head gesture. My daughters were so beautiful, and nothing could erase the immeasurable smiles which gleamed across their faces. Although, I couldn't help but notice that my son found it very difficult to look at me. At one point, his mother sent him to the vending machine. At that time she and my daughters told me that he was leery of coming here, and didn't know what to expect. When he returned, I sat him in the seat next to me, and I began to talk with him directly in an effort to assure him of the surroundings. He began to touch my hands and to rub my arms. In his soft monotone voice he said, *"Daddy, you don't look real!"* I chuckled, and quickly changed the subject realizing that the last physical memory they had of me was during the trial. During that time I was told that I resembled a terminally ill patient. My oldest daughter never ceased from staring at me. Silently, I wondered if she reflected back to the day when we held each other on her mother's porch. The entire time during our visit I fought to restrain the tears because I wanted this day to be anything but somber. It was beautiful! Life's simplest pleasures are in God's simplest blessings. Whether being bound or free; this was a day which I won't soon forget- if ever.

With the passing of several months, my younger daughter had also graduated from high school. My feelings of regret never remitted. On a particular day, my two daughters came alone to visit me once more. At one point during our visit, my younger daughter straightly asked, *"What happened that night Daddy?"* I knew that this question delved into their minds, and I realized then that without my candor before the parole board, I wouldn't be able to have this conversation in its truest form with my children. Without reservation, I sat with my daughters and told them about the events of that night. My older daughter then said to me, *"Daddy, even though you're in here, it's made you into the person that you are now. I mean, you have always been a good dad and a good person, but, even more so now that you've gone through this."* My younger daughter, who had just begun college, told me that her college roommate couldn't wait to meet me. Puzzled, I asked, *"Does she know about me? I mean, does she know where I am?"* My oldest daughter then exclaimed, *"Daddy, we're not ashamed of you! All of our friends who know you always ask about you. People who have known you, knows who you really are. And even though you are in here, it's like you aren't!"* I thank God for my children. For even in the midst of seeing my shame laid open bare naked, still, they love and reverence me none the less. It reads in Proverbs 30:18, 19:

> *There are three things which are too wonderful for me, yea, four which I know not: the way of an eagle in the air; the way of a serpent upon a rock; the way of a ship in the midst of the sea; and the way of a man with a maid.*

As for me, it's the love of my three children and the working ways of God that are far too wonderful for me. It's far more than I can ever begin to comprehend. For all four, I'm grateful. Soon after our visit, I received a heartfelt card from my daughter.

> *No matter how grown up I may be or how independent I feel, no matter the distance between us or the time between visits, no matter what happens today or tomorrow...there's one thing that you can always be sure of – and that's how much I love you Daddy!*

I heard a man once tell about how he categorizes people in his life as a tree. He explained that the leaves are those who are in your life that wither and blow away. The branches are those who appear to be in your corner, but as soon as a storm arises they snap and fall apart. Roots are those who will stand with you. They will hold you up and stand their ground no matter what storm may come. When I think about this analogy, for my life, I've had many leaves and some branches. However, my roots are deeply embedded with my children. Through them I understand that having someone in your corner is just as important as having them right by your side.

TRANQUILITY IN GOD

One evening, proceeding Monday night Bible study, I was approached by an inmate who, with no explanation, told me to read Psalm 32. Ergo, based on his suggestion, I sat up in my bed that night and read this chapter.

> Blessed is he whose transgression is forgiven, whose sin is covered. Blessed is the man unto whom the Lord imputeth not iniquity, and in whose spirit there is no guile. When I kept silence, my bones waxed old through my roaring all the day long. For day and night thy hand was heavy upon me: my moisture is turned into the drought of summer. I acknowledge my sin unto thee, and mine iniquity have I not hid, I said, I will confess my transgressions unto the Lord; and thou forgavest the iniquity of my sin. For this shall every one that is Godly pray unto thee in a time when thou mayest be found: surely in the floods of great waters they shall not come nigh unto him. Thou art my hiding place; thou shalt preserve me from trouble; thou shalt compass me about with songs of deliverance. I will instruct thee and teach thee in the way which thou shalt go; I will guide thee with with mine eye. Be ye not as the horse, or as the mule, which have no understanding: whose mouth must be held in with bit and bridle, lest they come near unto thee. Many sorrows shall be to the wicked: but he that trusteth in the Lord, mercy shall compass him about.

Be glad in the Lord, and rejoice, ye righteous: and shout
for joy, all ye that are upright in heart.

It was after I read this scripture that I understood this inmate's reasoning. The longer I kept silent and concealed the calamity of that fateful night, the more the fiber of my soul and spirit groaned. Therefore, as it reads in this scripture, I had to acknowledge my transgression. Through His infinite grace and mercy, God has forgiven me. He is my hiding place.

The following morning, once more, I was approached while working in the chapel. A young reception inmate, whom I've never seen before, came to me and said, *"You might want to read this."*

He handed me a letter, and then stood closely by as I read it. It was titled,

The Duck and the devil:

A little boy was visiting his grandparents on their farm. He was given a slingshot to play with out in the woods. He practiced in the woods, but he could never hit the target. While getting a little discouraged, he headed back for dinner. As he was walking back, he saw grandma's pet duck. Just out of impulse he let the slingshot fly and he hit the duck square in the head and killed it. He was shocked and grieved! In a panic, he hid the dead duck in the wood pile, only to see his sister watching. Sally had seen it all, but she said nothing. After lunch the next day, grandma said, 'Sally, let's wash the dishes.' But Sally said, 'Grandma, Johnny told me that he wanted to help in the kitchen.' Then she whispered to Johnny, 'Remember the duck!' So, Johnny did the dishes. Later that day, grandpa asked if the children wanted to go fishing, and grandma said, 'I'm sorry, but I need Sally to help me make supper.' Sally just smiled and said, 'Well, that's alright, because Johnny told me that he wanted to help.' She again whispered to Johnny,

'Remember the duck!' So Sally went fishing and Johnny stayed to help grandma. After several days of Johnny doing both his chores and Sally's, he finally couldn't stand it any longer! He came to grandma and confessed that he had killed the duck. Grandma knelt down, gave him a hug and said, 'Sweetheart, I know. You see, I was standing at the kitchen window and saw the whole thing, but because I love you, I forgave you! I was wondering how long you would let Sally make a slave of you.'

With this, I came to understand that God was letting me know that He saw the whole thing! And even with that, He forgave me. He was wondering how long I was going to allow my past to predict my future. With my confession, I will never again be held in servitude of my former self.

———◆———

One quiet morning, while buffing the floor of the chapel, an aura of quietness and tranquility happened to fill the room. Tears suddenly began to whelp in my eyes as I pondered on the goodness of God which began to overwhelm me. Subsequently, I sensed someone's presence, only to turn and see the chaplain standing there observing me. I had no idea the length of time he was there, or if he noticed my tears. However, he must have gathered the state of my essence because he said to me," *I know that you are taking this time that you have here to reflect. Believe it or not Luke, you will never have this alone time again. You are at so much peace right now."* And with that, he exited the chapel leaving me alone with my thoughts. I was taken aback when suddenly I thought about all that I had accomplished while being a State Trooper. I thought about the time and opportunity I had when escorting and standing side by side with, at that time, the future President of the United States. The time I was selected to provide security for the Vice President when a tornado ripped through my home town, and he came to view the damage. I reflected on the Secretary of State, and the many other dignitaries that I provided security for. But amazingly, all the accolades; all the reverence; all the respect; paled, to the peace I felt at that one solitary moment. These moments in time may have been my greatest accomplishments, yet, I believe that God is far more interested in who I am now, rather than the man that I was during my time of being a State Trooper. Because in reality, being a State Trooper is what I did, it's not who I was.

I heard a guest pastor who had spent time in prison speak one day in church service. *"My time in prison was some of the best times of my life. Because never again will I have the opportunity to get this close to God."* While holding and feeling the vibration of that buffer in my hands, amazingly, this was a choice moment of my life!

Later that same afternoon, I was called to the front desk by the officer who works in the education building. With a startled look he said, *"Luke, you need to report to the captain's office."* Next to being called to having to see the chaplain, no inmate wants to hear that they have to report to the captain's office. As I entered, I was met by two captains who said abruptly, *"Have a seat in the front lobby!"* I became troubled by an uncertainty as to what this was all about. Instantly, I was overridden with fear and anxiety. My agitation worsened when I heard the phone ring in the background and one of the captains came and asked me, *"Hey bud, what's your name?"* Timidly, I responded, *"McCormick."* He turned and yelled to the captain who had answered the phone, *"Yeah, we've got the right one!"* Sublime, in overwhelming horror, I thought, *"God help me! What's going on?"* Then suddenly, I observed a woman approaching the entrance of the captain's office. She entered, and came directly to where I was sitting. She shifted the paperwork in her arms, extended her hand to me and introduced herself as the warden's secretary. Obviously, because she saw the bewildered look on my face, she smiled and calmly assured me that I was not in trouble. She then explained to me the reason I was called to the captain's office. The institution, namely, the warden, received a call from a local news station in my home area. They wanted permission to come to the institution with a camera and conduct an interview with me. She then told me the name of the news station, and the anchor person who had contacted the warden. Instantly, thoughts tore through my mind of my time at the county jail, and this same anchor person from this news station was granted permission to conduct an interview with me. I recall the feeling of being startled as unexpectedly during that interview a bombshell of a question plummeted on me. I was asked during that time by the anchor woman if it was true that I came home the night of the incident and found my wife sleeping with another man. Incognizant, I was paralyzed and numbed to learn that this sentiment was the belief of many. To this day, my sister believes that subconsciously I've suppressed the true image of that night.

The warden's secretary then told me how the news anchor woman was unyielding in her efforts. She assured the institution staff I would know who she was. She explained to me that it was totally my decision as to whether I would grant the interview with this news station. Instantaneously, my thoughts immersed on my children. I thought about how seeing their father on television once more would impact their lives. With that thought in mind, unequivocally, I told the warden's secretary, *"Due to the situation and circumstance of all who are involved other than myself, I'm going to have to decline."* Lightly panting a sigh of relief, she kindly asked me to sign a form denying media access. While I signed the form, seeming subdued, she told me that she didn't blame me for not granting access for the interview because she too believed that they wanted to once again exploit me with one of those *"where are they now"* type of segments. For the next few days, I pondered about why the media wanted to interview me. I wondered, *"Was it because they had learned about my confession? Had they already interviewed my wife, and now wanted an exclusive about my side of the story?"* Whatever the reason, I couldn't once again fall victim and be the prey to satisfy the media's hunger. Soon after, I received a card from my oldest daughter which read:

From your daughter Dad...

Yours are the hands that raised me, and guided me when
I was small – that lifted me to laugh at the sky, and held

me when I was hurt or afraid. Yours is the voice I could recognize even before I could talk – the voice that could calm me, comfort me, quite my fears with just a single word. Yours are the eyes I look into, that could say so much to me with just a glance – that could see through me and into me... eyes that have smiled at me and with me through all the years, in good times and bad. Then and now, you are the Dad I've always loved and I always will, so very much. I will always be your baby.

My daughter has helped me to understand, that no matter what, I'll always be that special someone in her eyes. Though everything in me wants for the world to know that the events of that night didn't happen in the way that it's portrayed, yet still, her card made me realize that there are too many other casualties for me to consider. One night, I read Psalm 17:3 which summarized my convictions to their entirety.

Thou hast proved mine heart; thou hast visited me in the night; thou hast tried me, and shalt find nothing; I am purposed that my mouth shall not transgress.

With this, I pray, *"Lord, let nothing of my past be found in me!"* In this I proclaim.

IT'S WHAT 'HE' THINKS THAT MATTERS

Astrange occurrence took place one afternoon while I was eating lunch in the chow hall. The officer who was assigned there that day said to me, *"McCormick, I need to talk to you when you're finished eating!"* Instantly, I felt a wall envelop me. I knew that he had fixated on his mind to pursue a conversation about the highway patrol. I dumped my tray and went to the table where he sat and stood facing him. Immediately, without hesitation he delved into his questions. *"You were a State Trooper right?"* I knew this to be a rhetorical question, however, I responded, *"Yes."* In deferring to get to the validity of his quest to talk with me he asked, *"Does the Highway Patrol have quotas? Why do you see more Troopers out on some days as compared to others?* And, *"How long were you a Trooper?"* Finally, after my response to his barrage of questions and bantering he asked a very candid and pointed one, which I thought to be his main objective. He asked, *"How much time did they give you?* His countenance took on a new form, and he appeared to be disgusted when I responded, *"Ten years."* He deeply offended me and evoked me to anger when he quickly replied, *"Do you think that ten years was enough?"* It took every ounce of strength in me to compose myself and refrain from a verbal retort! In restraint, I responded, *"When you take into account that incarcerated here within this institution are men who have committed murder, only to have these charges reduced to* *manslaughter causing them to only serve three to five years – 'Yes!' I think that my ten years is more than sufficient to fit my crime!"* He took notice of my anger and sat quietly before he asked, *"Do you regret it?"* Poignantly, I responded, *"Do I regret the job, or do I regret what occurred?"* With his face distorted because of my response, he replied, *"Do you regret what you did? I mean, I can only imagine. I'm not trying to be smart, but you must have really hit rock bottom for this to have happened to you. It just doesn't fit your personality at all!"* For the next few moments, it seemed that the chow hall became vacant. The only voice that I heard was my own amplifying. I told this officer, *"Not one single day goes by that I don't regret my actions of that night. As profoundly remorseful as I am, what I did to my wife is something that will haunt me for the rest of my life."* With a sense of appeasement, the C.O. simply said with a smile, *"Okay McCormick, you take care."* I walked away not knowing his true intentions. However, I hope that from his personal inquiry about me, he understands that no matter what your position is in society, you're not immune to *life* happening to you. To find yourself incarcerated is the most deplorable circumstance that a man could ever find himself to be in. Yet, for me, somehow - someway, just as the chaplain once told me, I'm all the better for it!

I made a mistake one day during a visit by asking my mother a question. I have one sister out of four who never visits, never writes, and to the best of my knowledge never even asks about me. So, one day during a visit, I asked my mother, *"Why?"* I requested for her implacable honesty because at this point, feelings are not an issue. She paused before saying, *"I haven't been told directly, but she's mad and upset because she can't understand how you did this – how you let this happen to yourself. She said she knows if she were to ever come home, she's going to feel pressured to come and visit you. She doesn't understand how we do it – how we come and just sit in this depressing place."* Silence filled the room momentarily as my sister, brother-in-law, and I digested what we just heard. Calmly, I thanked my mother for her honesty when hurt suddenly transpired as

I told her, *"Mom, when I do come home, and I see her for the first time,"* I paused; *"I just don't know. I honestly just don't know."* I fought back tears as a part of me already knew the answer – I knew she harbored ill feelings towards me in regard to me because I'm in prison. However, I guess the other part of me needed to hear it.

The following Sunday morning in church, the pastor was teaching from Psalm 51, and as he spoke, verses one, four, and seven resonated within my heart and spirit. They read:

> *Have mercy upon me, O God, according to thy loving kindness: according unto the multitude of thy tender mercies blot out my transgressions. Wash me thoroughly from mine iniquity, and cleanse me from my sin. For I acknowledge my transgressions: and my sin is ever before me. Against thee, thee only, have I sinned, and done this evil in thy sight: that thou mightest be justified when thou judgest. Purge me with hyssop, and I shall be clean: wash me, and I shall be whiter than snow.*

In going through all that I have, I now know that the Lord allowed it in order to heal me of all the pretense, foolishness, and worldliness in me. If He had not put His fear in my heart – if I hadn't had to deal with these issues of my life, I wouldn't be who I am today. So as my sister decides within herself to judge me and my actions which led to my incarceration, I turn my hurt towards this scripture. It's against God that I have sinned, and it's because of God that I've been forgiven, no matter what her feelings are towards me. God knew all along what was in my heart, and He knew exactly how to get my attention. If I didn't see the Lord working in my circumstances, or if I didn't believe the steps of the righteous are ordered by His hand – then my faith, my life, would have gone crashing to the ground. I think again of the time the Chaplain asked me, *"How do you stop a runaway train? You derail it."* When I think of the comments from my sister I'm reminded of Psalm 66:10, 12:

For thou, O God, hast proved us: thou has tried us, as silver is tried. We went through fire and through water: but thou broughtest us out into a wealthy place.

My sister knows nothing tangible about me or what I've gone through. I've went through the fire, and been through the flood; but God delivered me through it all. I was living a life that was not true to anyone, first and foremost myself. But something since has transpired within me, and God has molded me into a new vessel. It's been as though He has said, *"Luke, let me love you through this, I want you to get to know Me in the midst of this. I'm using this to show you the depths of My love."* I remember a friend here once telling me, *"God is using this time so you can get closer to Him."* If my sister or anyone else can't understand that though it may hurt, I can't hold onto or focus on their feelings or reservations towards me. Whatever the reason may be, she is making this about me, though I believe it runs deeper than that. I believe it factors more on hidden issues within her own life. Ironically, I received a card from a loving cousin who always seems to know when to send the perfect words. The card read:

> *Sometimes it's so hard to put the past behind us...We'll remember something, and before we know it, our spirits start to sink again. But you know what? The past is old business that's over and done with. But your future is a whole different matter. You have the right to be happy, and you have the power to start shaping your life into what you want it to be. You are a strong person and I know what you're capable of once you make up your mind. I know that your future is going to be wonderful. You deserve nothing less than living "happily ever after."*

I refuse to let my past haunt me any longer. I want to be sensitive to God and to always seek to be pleasing in His sight. In the midst of my affliction, God has given me *marvelous* and *wonderful* revelations, and He has spoken all of this to me – not with a resounding voice, but deep within my heart.

A VOICE FROM
THE PAST

As the days and months slowly drift away my heart becomes increasingly lonelier for the desire to love someone and to have that *special* someone in my life. Two years have passed since my divorce, although emotionally, I've been alone for a long time. In fact, I heard a pastor say something that related so much to my life. *"People think the divorce was final when your received the legal document of decree, but you've been divorced emotionally a long time ago."* I look back over my life of shattered dreams, broken promises and bad relationships, and I often wonder if it's meant to be for me. I think of my promiscuous life, and I can't help but wonder if somehow God is punishing me for the mistakes of my past because He did not bring that special someone into my life. I've plead with God many lonely nights; I've shed many tears, and yet, I'm so lonely. I feel so isolated. So many times I've wanted to do as it says in Psalm 55:6... *"Oh, that I had wings like a dove! I would fly away and be at rest."*

I recall one night back in 2004, when I was in prayer, confessing my all to God. My father had just passed away a few months earlier, and it took me a long time to recover from that. To this day, I still haven't had my moment to mourn, and this one particular night, I laid it all out before the Lord.

As I poured out my heart and confessed my faults to Him, a face appeared to me. It was the face of someone in my past. The portrait that captured my mind's eye was my first love and childhood sweetheart. And then, in a still small voice, I heard these words: *"Whom you will marry."* With tears streaming down my cheeks, my words, and my prayer silenced. I listened. I thought, *"What was that?"* All the while knowing it was God's voice because I had heard it before and each time, it came the same way. This picture He brought to me, came not only as I was confessing and repenting from my past relational errors, but she arrived when I surrendered my being and life to the Gracious one. It occurred to me, *"I haven't seen this girl for over thirty years! I don't know anything about her or her life."* All I could remember was that she was in the Air Force. I knew nothing else, and honestly began to question those four words I'd just heard. But again, I knew it was God.

Years passed and still, I was empty, isolated and alone. More lonely than I've ever been in my entire life. One day my baby sister sent a book to me that she said *literally* jumped off the shelf at her feet when she was in a Christian book store. She had previously spoken to me about this book, saying that I really needed to read it. It's about a Christian couple, who waited and trusted God to intervene in their life paths to send them their future spouse. *Oh!* This story blessed me beyond words. It communicated a hope and desire that only the soul could comprehend. As I immersed my being in the details of this couples faith journey, words didn't have the power to convey the message I received. Their story, their total trust and dependence upon God to write the love story of their lives, devoted my heart to do the same. With the inspiration from this book, an expression of trust and love, I routinely prayed three things daily. *"Lord, if it's Your will for me to ever be married again, and spend my earthy days with a partner, then I trust You to choose her for me. I'm willing to be single, and the next woman I date will be my wife."* Once this prayerful petition became part of my being, those four words spoken to me never returned, until one day I received a card, and the words said; *"I guess you could say this is a voice from your past."* My heart simultaneously smiled and sunk. It was her! My first girlfriend! My very first love!

As the weeks and months passed, she and I corresponded more frequently, and with the receipt of each letter, something churned within my heart; something I'd never felt before. I learned that she was still in the Air Force, and she was stationed in Maryland. Though she had been in the service for many years, all I could picture was that cute little girl from Church Street where we grew up. I recall once on a visit, my mom asked me if I had ever really loved anyone. The first and only name that came to me instantly, without reservation, was hers. Just as it was the night I heard those four words, secretly I thought, *"What was that?"* Little did I know that she had never left me. Her memory...the memory of her; never ever left me.

I began to notice a pattern. Each time I would pray those three statements from the book, I would receive a letter from her, and I'd hear a certain song on the radio which spoke about trusting the Lord. I began to secretly ask my family questions about her without them knowing my reasoning for inquiring. I would tell my mom every time I'd receive a letter from her, but it took an extreme effort from me to conceal my heart. This woman *excited* me with every letter and every word she wrote to me. My mind and heart was overwhelmed and going places I'd never known before. Her letters *mesmerized* me, and suddenly, I was insatiable. I hadn't spoken to her in years, let alone seen her; yet, I was smitten by her and couldn't control it, even if I tried. Suddenly, I felt like a little boy again. In all of my years, only she has made me feel this way. My single most desire was to run back to the pod every day from work with the hope that a letter was waiting for me. I simply couldn't get enough of her now. My need to be close to her was insatiable.

To my dismay, I learned that not all her letters would comfort me. Deployment to Iraq was the content of one letter. My heart was filled with terror, though I never shared this with her. We continued our correspondence, and with each letter, without much being said – much was being said. I could feel her so much through her words, and though it had been so many years since we were girlfriend and boyfriend, *still*, I knew her so well. This was the most *natural* feeling I had ever felt. How I wanted to express so much to her. I wanted to share and give my all to her so freely, and I couldn't contain it. I also couldn't control it.

A few weeks passed and I hadn't received any letters from her. My mom had formed an intimate relationship with her, and would inquire about my communication with her. My response was, *"No,"* with a hidden brokenness in my heart. I began to worry due to her deployment in Iraq. The world news became daily viewing for me, with the hope that I might get a glimpse of her. I became increasingly concerned, when one day my mother told she had talked with her mother. I learned that our mothers were in a community choir together, and she had sent a message through her mom to tell me that she was in some sort of transition. She didn't want me to think she had forgotten me, and even wanted to send me a picture. I imagined that she was as cute as she always had been. A couple weeks later I received a picture of her, and my intuition was correct. Someone so cute and so sweet never changed. She was still that cute little girl I was in love with many years ago.

I spent many day and nights gazing at her picture. I remembered every part of her face. My memories were filled with the days and nights of our childhood. She in my parents basement, and I in her mother's living room. *Oh!* How I wanted to return to those times. Lord knows, I'd give anything to go back.

<hr>

As Christmas time drew near, I thought about what life in Iraq was like for her. I wondered if the same anguishes I felt, being absent from my family, was the same she felt. My intuition told me I was right. Somehow, it seemed that our experiences aligned and yet, no explanation adequately explained this phenomenon. I just know that I did. As miserable as my situation was being away from my family, and this being my favorite time of year, I felt worse for her. I wished her to be with her family more than myself.

Again, time passed, and no letter. I worried. My every thought was now consumed by her. Then, one day I received a letter from her that stated she was at last coming home at the end of January. She also said that she would like to visit, which both excited me beyond words and made me nervous. I hadn't seen her for years, and I wondered what we would talk about, and if there would be awkward moments. My heart fluttered with the thought of seeing her again. Her visitation date was the 9th of February. Little did I know that this would be a day that would revolutionize my life forever.

When the 9th finally arrived, the butterflies were doing the jig in my stomach. I had tried for days to rehearse words and conversations to share with her, but nothing prepared me for when I walked in that visiting room and saw the most *beautiful* sight I've ever seen. There she was with her back to me, and at that moment it was as if the heavens parted and everything I'd ever gone through in my life suddenly had meaning, with just one glimpse of her. It was as though I could hear the voice of God telling me, *"This is what you've gone through all your life for."* As we embraced, my childhood came rushing back to me. With her arms wrapped around me, I felt something I felt only once before, back in her mother's living room on the corner of Church and Orchard. We talked, we laughed and we shared so much. It was as though our worlds had never parted. It was like we never left each other. I kept saying to her, *"I can't believe you're here!"* I sat in that visiting room looking at the *most* beautiful sight I'd ever seen, the most beautiful sight I remember from so long ago. *"My God!"* she was beautiful. I couldn't resist her, even if I tried. Her eyes, her smile, her laugh, everything about her captivated me. This day was the best day of my existence. It was the best I had ever felt in my entire life. We really were giddy teens on our first date for the second time, from so long ago. We shared a soda and a sandwich, and sharing the same soda seemed so natural. Everything about us that day seemed so natural, like it and us, were meant to be. We shared so much in those hours that we sat there together, and no part of my life was off limits to her. I felt vulnerable, yet safe at the same time. Even though it has been years since we had seen each other, I wanted to conceal nothing from her. I wanted to tell her my all. I felt I could be totally transparent with her, and I wanted to be. How badly I wanted to tell her at that moment, *"One day, you are going to be my wife."* It took all I had to refrain from uttering that sentiment, yet, somehow, I felt if I had said it that she would have understood. I felt our intuitive knowledge of one another was that intimate. In the time of this visit, she knew more about me than any woman ever has. More than anyone ever will.

As this day came to an end and the C.O. yelled out that visiting was over, we stood and embraced. As I held her in my arms, I whispered to her, *"Thank you for coming."* She told me that she was glad that she did, and at that moment I wanted to kiss her. I wanted to kiss her so badly. I watched the movement of her body as she walked toward the door. I wanted to remember every part of her that day. I didn't want to forget one single moment. I caught her warm brown eyes as she walked down the walkway; my full attention wondered when I would see this *magnificent* creature again. When would I once again be blessed with such a day as this? 9 February, 2008, the day my life changed forever more.

⊰◆⊱

Exuberance and joy filled me as I anticipated the moment when I could craft my next letter. My mind and heart were so full of emotions, and I wanted her to know them all. I told her of the joy she brought to me that day, about how it was the absolute *best* day I've ever had in my entire life. I told her everything, without reservation. There was nothing in my heart that I wanted to withhold from her. Vulnerable or not, I wanted to be an open book to her. For her to know all of me. From Church Street to this moment, I wanted her to reacquaint with me all over again. As I sat in my bed writing to my very first love, I wondered if she felt the same as I did, and wondered if she felt the depth of chemistry flowing between us that day. I wondered, too, would she write and share her all with me.

That question was answered a few days later when I received a letter from her that was written the same night as our visit. Tears of joy filled my eyes and heart, as she explained how she felt that day. It was the same as me. I knew God was up to something, something very wonderful and true. Something unlike anything I'd ever experienced in my life.

As the calendar pages turned, she and I became very close all over again. With each visit, letter and phone conversation, I became increasingly entranced with her. I found myself *longing* for each time I got to see her, talk with her and read the beautiful writing of her words. I latched onto each and every word she wrote to me, and my grip could not be unclenched. It absolutely *fascinated* me that her hands touched this paper that I held now in my hands. I smelled each letter and each word with the hope that I would catch her scent. Everything about her *penetrates* me! Penetrates me in ways so unimaginable. Each day I waited for a letter and each week I ached to hear her soft voice; and each month, I longed to behold her beautiful face. She and I had become one. I simply couldn't resist it, nor did I want to. There was nothing about me that I didn't want to share with her. Through our talks, she came to know things about me, that before, only God knew. I often remember things I've experienced in my life. I believe now that it all led me to her. For me to be able to appreciate all of her, just as she is. I believe when this all happened with me coming to prison, from that moment God began preparing me for her. He prepared me once again for my first love. God had begun to purge me and make me pure for her. It's as though He put me to sleep to create in me – her. My crucifixion and my prison were not complete until He returned her back to me. My crucifixion was for her; she has made me complete. He's brought everything full circle and back to my beginning, only this time I plan on getting it right. She is my beginning. This time, it's forever.

One day during a phone conversation, I felt an urgency to tell her what had been lying so heavily upon my heart since the first time I laid my eyes on her in the visiting room. While I struggled, due to fear of her reaction, she said to me, *"Would it help if I said I love you?"* It was then that I knew this was of God, and it was then that I told her, *"I'm falling in love with you, all over again."*

I received a card from her one day, and like all of our correspondence, it had the words I've held secretly within my heart for years. Until now; until her; I've never let them be known. The card read:

> *You're my love and my best friend...and the friendship we share makes the love and the romance between us means even more to me. Our relationship is so much richer and*

more fulfilling, and I feel a special peace and comfort when I'm with you. It's like you soothe my soul as well as excite me in so many ways. I always wanted to be friends with the person I fell in love with. I always felt that was important somehow, and now I know why. Knowing that you're there for me to lean on whenever I have a problem, and knowing I can do the same for you... makes me feel incredibly lucky. I know that not every couple feels such deep friendship for each other...and it feels my heart with even more love for you to know that we share something so special.

I've always told myself that I wanted my lover to also be my best friend. Someone to whom I could not only love with all my heart, but trust her with the same. I know now I have that in her. She is my calm, my peace and my serenity. She truly is all and everything I've ever dreamed of, hoped for, and ever desired. She not only is my best friend, but also my spiritual partner; my wingman, and my *most precious* love. She is truly a rare jewel that God placed in my life all over again. Never before have I felt a love that transcends death. Never before has there been a woman in my life that I would give my very life for. She soothes every part of me. She brings comfort to my very existence.

━━◆━━

I was in church service the weekend before Father's day, when I was told by the C.O. that I had a visit. I entered the visiting room and observed my children sitting there along with their mother. This was a sight my aching eyes have waited for, for such an elongated time. I was mindful of them as their eyes were fixed on me, calculating my every step to the C.O.s' desk. One by one we embraced, and the emotions of my heart riveted between a mixture of joy and sorrow. *OH!* How I've missed them so! The essence of their embrace struck the very core of my soul. They told me they came this weekend because they would be out of town on Father's day, and through our conversations, we seemed to catch up on a lot of lost time. The closeness my children felt, in spite of

113

where I am, astonished me. It seems as though other than the absence of my physical presence, their lives have gone along uninterrupted. Looking within their eyes, their hearts, and every word they spoke, I found no shame within them. There was no embarrassment; just Daddy. And we love him in spite of. This was the best Father's day gift I can remember ever receiving from my children. Certainly, it's one that I'll never forget.

The following Sunday on Father's day, I received a visit from my very first love. She is the sweetest and most thoughtful person I know because she wanted to surprise me so I wouldn't be alone on this day. I often ask myself, *"Who am I? Who am I to deserve and receive such love and care from so many?"* It's hard for me to fathom and comprehend such fidelity. She also told me of a surprise she had in store for me within the next few days. I received mail from her which astounded me and brought weighty tears to my eyes. Because she knows the profound anguish I carry because I'm not able to see my grandmother due to her health she went to the nursing home and took pictures of her for me. She doesn't even know my grandmother – has never laid eyes on her, yet for me, she did this! Never, ever, has something meant so much! I shed an abundance of tears this day as a picture of she and my grandmother glistened in my eye. I loved this woman more now than ever before just from this one gesture of thoughtfulness. This meant more to me than I believe I could ever try to explain. No kinder act has ever been bestowed upon me; and none ever will.

The following week my mother and stepfather came to visit me, and I was told of my grandmother being very ill, so much so that my mother said Hospice had been called in for her. I fought back tears as I became disquieted because I didn't, or couldn't comprehend this news. It was just a few days ago that I received pictures of my grandmother and love, and she looked to be so vibrant and full of life, with the biggest smile beaming on her face. My world was then pulverized by my stepfather saying, *"She did that for you son."* My head dropped, and this time my attempt to swallow back tears faded, as they streamed down my face like a river to the visiting room floor. I wept bitterly. It seemed as though in some mystical way my love knew this event was about to transpire and befall upon me. It had been placed upon her loving heart for me to see my grandmother one last time, with a smile on her face.

The following weekend my grandmother passed away. My baby sister and her husband came to see me, and with one glance into her eyes I said, *"What?"* Tears whelped up in her eyes as she quietly and softly told me of grandma's passing at about 6:00 am that same morning. I was alright for a minute or two, but suddenly, I couldn't contain the dam of emotion, and I broke; and the river of tears flowed.

Through my tears I had my brother-in-law to ask the C.O. if I could go to the back room of the visiting area in an attempt to confine my emotions. The officer, being very understanding told me to take all the time I needed. I paced in this back lobby area and cried my eyes out, till I felt I had no tears left within me; then I cried some more. *Oh!* How my soul ached! I hadn't felt such pain since the passing of my father – and just as with him, I wasn't able to be there. I again felt in some way to be the cause of their grief, heartache, and affliction. Somehow, I felt that if I could have only been there, this wouldn't have happened, even though I know their very lives were in God's hands. Still, I somehow felt to be at fault, and this would be a grief I'd have to bare.

⟫◆⟪

I wrote a letter to my grandmother that I wanted to be read during her funeral. In my own words, this was my way of saying good bye.

A Grandmothers' Love:

I besought the Lord every single day, and asked Him to allow me the opportunity to spend quality time with you, outside of these prison walls. To walk you around Shawnee Park, or simply just to sit with you, and to be in your presence. But I guess this was not God's will, and it hurts me to the very core of my heart. Every time I would feel low because I felt I had let you and my family down… without you ever even knowing this, I'd receive a card from you telling me you loved me, and how proud you are to have me as your grandson. And though I could never understand how, due to my situation, I knew you meant it, and God knows I desperately needed to hear it. You've been an inspiration to me grandma, and I'm going to miss those *cards, those words, but most of all I'm going to miss you. I'm going to miss my grandma's love. Though I know the Lord has called you home, it still hurts none the less for not taking that walk in the park with you. I love you grandma, and I miss you so much. You've taken care of so many throughout your life…it's now time for the angels to take care of you.*

Your loving grandson…

It seems only a week earlier that I was in the chapel helping another inmate clean after Catholic service when a C.O. approached me and began sharing with me about his son who had recently been killed in a car accident. I had a sensibility that it was meant for me to quietly and attentively listen to him. I had no idea why he wanted to talk with me, but I was there, and I hearkened to the hurts and pains he spoke from within his heart. In spite of our two totally different worlds of circumstances, I was there for him. For that moment of time, he was not a C.O., and I not an inmate, but rather that listening ear he so desperately needed. And now, one week removed, here I am with the same need as this officer the only difference being that I have no one here to turn to. I often wonder, *"When is it going to be my turn to mourn? I hurt – I cry, and it's as though no one here's me."* Since being incarcerated, I've had to grow up in so many ways, and much of this growth has been through agony of affliction. This situation is no different. It seems the Lord had me in the chapel at that appointed time to be there for this C.O., while also preparing me for the hurt I was about to experience. The only exception being, that *He* is the one to listen to the cries and incoherent utterances of my heart. I've lost not only a grandmother, but a confidante who faithfully wrote to me each week.

Through this incarcerated pilgrimage, I've endured many a heartache and pain; but through it all, He remains my hope for tomorrow. Luke 6:21 reads; *"Blessed are ye that weep now: For ye shall laugh."* I want my smile back.

⟫◆⟪

Two weekends removed from my grandmothers' passing, I sat in my cell waiting for the officer to call me for my visit with my family. While waiting, the strangest thing happened to me, as I felt the strongest urge and tugging within my heart to pray. I had no inclination as to this drive within me, but I sat in my cell and simply prayed what was on my heart, which happened to be the love of my life. This short supplication didn't seem as it was me going before God for her, but rather, Him coming to me – for me. It felt as though He was tenderly holding and caressing my heart within His hands, yet still, I knew not why. My understanding was made clear when I went on my visit. While sitting there looking at my mother, sister and brother-in-law, I could perceive that I was about to once again receive some disturbing news. My mother looked at me with implicated eyes as she proceeded to tell me about a man, who had always been dear to me, had committed suicide. I was taken aback, and for a moment, I sat in disbelief. With barely enough time to absorb this, I again looked at my mother, and she suddenly appeared to be heavyhearted, and this weight she carried was for me. I felt it. My brother-in law then asked, *"Are you going to tell him or do you want me to?"* Agitation and anxiety impetuously rushed through my veins as I waited to hear what my mother's heart didn't want to tell me. What was it that she couldn't bear to say to add to the burden of her son's already befuddled heart? With tears in her eyes, she told me that my love received an assignment to go to Egypt. And with that, I now realize the reason He placed it upon my heart to pray. It was to prepare me for this moment.

I held strong momentarily, realizing she and I had just spoken the day before of this possibility. But now it has become reality. Then all at once and unannounced, the levy of my heart broke, and the flood of tears flowed. It was too much! This was just too much! My mother felt my anguish; it was depicted in the tears streaming down her face. My sister, being mindful said, *"She's crying for you."* OH! Why does it have to hurt so badly? I'm aching beyond comprehension with all I've had to endure over these past few weeks, *"I'm trying Lord! I'm trying to stay strong, but I honestly don't know how much more I can take!"* I just don't know. It feels as though my heart is bleeding, and my only tourniquet is leaving to go to another country. Only she can stop this pain which flows through me like a watercourse.

The following Sunday afternoon I was at the gym working out when unexpectedly the C.O. yelled to me that I had a visit. I scurried back to the pod and showered, all the while wondering who it was that had come to see me. I was hopeful of it being my love, though I knew otherwise, because she was in Indiana attending her family reunion. But as I walked into the visiting room, my eyes hushed my heart, for there she was, sitting with her legs crossed underneath her with the warmest smile on her face. *Ah!* We wilted into each other's arms, as all else around and within us disintegrated. Ultimately, after losing our clasp on one another, she reached across the table and wiped droplets of sweat from my brow, as tears whelped within both of our eyes. I asked joyfully as a little child, *"What are you doing here? I thought you were in Indiana?"* With a mixture of sadness, joy and pain across her face, she explained to me that she had spoken with my mother the night before, and learned of my reaction to the news of her assignment to Africa. It was at that moment that I'd realized she came home for me. It was also at that moment that I realized I loved her more than anything. I had an inverse of emotions as I thought of this being the opportunity of a lifetime for her, but also the dreariest moment of a lifetime for me. I didn't want her to go; but how could I be so selfish as to implore her to stay. We discussed and rehearsed the good in this assignment, but deep within, nothing of it made sense to my heart. I only knew that I wanted so desperately for her not to depart.

I woke early the following Monday morning just after my cell mate left for work. It was about 5:20 am, and I sat on my bunk gazing out of my cell window at the darkened sky, which was fitting because it embodied the interior of my heart. I wondered why things often turn out the way that they do in life, and pondered why my current situation hasn't changed. And once again, tears flowed with the thought of her leaving. The words to a song began to resonate within the core of my soul. It was as though the Spirit of God began whispering this chorus to me. The song was titled, *"The Battle is not yours, it's the Lord's."* I climbed down from my bunk and went to my knees, and with my hands raised I pleaded with the Creator, *"I need you Lord! I can't do this alone! How do I stop this pain? How do I stop the continual drops of tears from raining upon my face?"* At times I think I'm all cried out when the real truth of the matter is my heart is full of tears. I wonder how many more will be shed before this segment of my lifetime is curtailed. For now, I'm left searching the secret recesses of my soul for a hidden strength to alleviate this imprisoned pain dwelling within me.

Later this same morning while at my job in the education department, I was sitting behind my computer when a *still* small voice spoke to the ears of my heart; *"Don't you see God moving?"* I stopped what I was doing as a sudden peace resided over me. As I did once before, I felt my heart being held by God, and Him telling me *"Everything is going to be okay – only trust Me."*

The most thoughtful gesture occurred when I returned to the pod after work. There on my bunk was two packs of twizzlers candy with a note that read; *"My wife and I just wanted you to have a little of your favorite. Enjoy and keep your head up."* This was from a friend of mine who I have helped through some difficult times. He learned of my misfortunes from my mother talking with him during visits, and because he knows this is my favorite candy, he and his wife ordered it for me through a food box. Something so trivial to others meant more to me at that moment than he could ever imagine. It proved to me that no matter what I go through during this journey, God is going to be right there with me, no matter how great or small the circumstance. At that point, I dropped my head, closed my eyes, and whispered within my heart, *"Lord don't just change my situation, but also change me through it. Lord, help me to stand!"* Through this I've learned that sometimes it's the little things that can bring such joy and pleasure in life.

BACK TO COURT

E arly one Monday morning, I had just sat down in the chow hall for breakfast when another inmate came to my table, leaned in close and whispered, *"I don't know if you already know this, but the C.O. at the pod was calling for you to pack it up because you're going back to court."* I waited for him to smile and tell me that he was joking, but when I saw the seriousness on his face, my stomach submerged and my appetite instantaneously subsided.

I hastened back to the pod and was met by the C.O. who told me to pack my belongings because they just called for me to go out to court. I went to my cell with my only thoughts being, *"This is it! God, this is the moment I've been waiting and believing for! My miracle has finally come to pass!"* In the process of me gathering my things, as is custom, I noticed several inmates looking up to my cell, trying to figure out what was going on. Anytime there is movement of any sort from the normal, all else is relinquished, and inquisitiveness seizes all. There was no deviation this day with me, and through all their delving and inquisitiveness, I was just as confounded as they were. My cell mate hearing of this came back from work to help me pack my things. I think a part of him also wondered what was going on, and though everyone else was inquiring, he merely helped me pack in quietness. Other inmates approached, hugging me, shaking my hand, and telling me good luck. These gestures solely heightened my appetite and thirst for these to be the last steps I traipse through this pod, and within the confines and grounds of this institution. While walking to the vault to secure my belongings, several staff members inquired as to where I was going. My answer was the same as it was with the inmates at the pod, *"All I know is that I'm going back to court."* In sincerity they said, *"Good luck to you."*

Upon arriving at the vault, and just as the first day of my arrival, I was stripped of my dignity by being strip searched. I donned an orange jump suit and was secluded in a holding cell, while I waited for the Montgomery County Sheriff's Department to transfer me back to court. Hours passed, and in spite of my ambience, my mind traveled throughout the atmosphere. I thought only of home.

When the deputy from the Sheriff's Department arrived, I noticed that he had transported other inmates from the county jail. I reflected back to the day I arrived. It seemed to be so long ago, yet, like only yesterday. The shackles and chains were secured on my wrists, ankles and waist, and I shuffled to the van. This too, was a mirror of my past. I thought the most frightening periods of my life were buried behind these memories, but little did I know, that what I was about to go through eclipsed any foregoing experience.

Prior to exiting the prison grounds, the deputy stopped the van so the guard at the back gate could search it. I straightway recognized this C.O.; he was the same one that spoke to me when I arrived on my first day. He assured that I'd be safe in his pod. I couldn't help but find it ironic that he'd be the last to see me depart. He opened the van door to secure the inside, and as he saw me he asked, "where you going man?" I told him that I was going back to court, but didn't know why, and he said to me, *"If you get out, I'll meet you at the fishing bank – the first beer is on me!"* We drove through the prison gates, and I closed my eyes. I silently prayed that this would be my definitive image of this institution. I felt as though I was in a type of twilight zone as everything seemed new to me – like seeing everything for the first time, yet, all over again. I didn't look back to the prison grounds. I only absorbed what was before me. I felt tears forming as my eyes canvassed and scrutinized the channel sights before me. I wanted to see it all, and not miss a single thing. Creations looked so differently to me – *such* a whole new world! During my time of incarceration, I've attained a unique perspective on life, and things pertaining to it.

My excitement started to build as my home county drew near. The aspect of coming home...being home, became undeniable to me. There in that County Sheriff's van, I gazed out the window as the scenery of familiar things began to come into view, and the conduit of my heart responded. I noticed a few times the deputy peering at me through the rear view mirror, and I wondered if he somehow knew who I was, or if he just marveled at the way I seemed to notice everything so precisely. I wondered too if he noticed the single tear drop that wandered down my face, as the thought of many years ago when I patrolled this precise stretch of highway exuded the levee of my memory.

Upon arrival at the county jail, a recollection of time past seeped through my veins. While waiting to be processed, I retained the memory of that one single day, from so many years ago. Being mindful, I sat in the waiting area and reflected as I saw the isolated cell I once was held in with a pyramid of tears surging down my face. I thought about that dreadful phone call I made to my sister as I cried and pleaded for help. The Lord has *truly* brought me a long way since that time, though the thought of that somber day has never left me. It never will. And now it appears my life has gone full – circle, and just as it was that day, the feeling of loneliness again began to overwhelm me. Only this time, I felt much stronger and better equipped to theorize the affair before me.

Several hours passed before I was able to make my one allotted phone call which I made to my mother. I tried to explain to her why I was brought back to court when realistically I was as dumbfounded as she was. All I knew was that during my processing the deputy told me that I was back for what was called re-sentencing on my charge of felonious assault. I understood that I couldn't receive any further time, so to me – to us, *this* was it! This was the miracle we had so desperately been praying and waiting for! After speaking with my mother, I was moved to another holding area, and the harsh portrait of confinement suddenly became authentic to me in ways I never before thought imaginable. I was placed in a room with approximately one hundred other men from all walks of life, and the stench was grotesque. Like a herd of cattle grazing men were laying all over the cold concrete floor, and there I stood in the midst of them. An argument and fight ensued when one guy through a holding cell door, urinated on another guy as he rested by leaning his back against the wall. This being the jail I was processed through, and the fact that law enforcement seems to be hated more in the county jail system than prisons, I began to silently pray, *"Please don't let any of these guys recognize me from years ago on the news."* My face was a constant with the media, and the last thing I needed was for anyone in this room to point me out. Yet, in no wise, one of them identified me, not from my past, but as being incarcerated at the Corrections Reception Center. Oddly, I became a sort of icon to these hundreds of men in this room; an emblem of their hereafter. Imprisonment is in no way a badge of honor to me; but in the midst of men whom I've never met before, the mere notion of my incarceration acquired me instant respect that I couldn't fathom. All I could think was, *"If they could only conceive my background."*

This long-drawn-out night went on until finally a deputy called my name with several others. We were being taken to the bed area, and I couldn't wait to lay my head down from this exhausting, unbelievable day. Upon arriving to the cell area, all thoughts of sleep vanished in an instant! I was placed in a cell which held twelve men, and right away I deduced that all of them were over the age of twenty. Because it now had to be about two in the morning, there were no lights on, though I felt the heat of many eyes watching my every move. I just wanted to make my bunk just enough for me to wilt into the mattress. In order to accomplish this feat, I had to reach above the guy below me, and then, in the dark, I heard a voice say from the bottom bunk, *"What's going on old school?"* Once more, I was recognized from someone who had previously been incarcerated at the Corrections Reception Center. We briefly talked, albeit I was depleted. Just as I seemed to have collapsed on this cold, hard bunk, my system went into shock as I was awakened to rapping, singing, arguing, and yelling! Paralyzed, I laid looking straight at the ceiling, awe stricken and taken aback by what my ears were hearing! I said not a word; I couldn't, for fear of the aftereffects, as this seemed to be a momentous occasion for all of these young guys. It was like this display was a nightly ritual that I was now in the center of. *All night!* This boisterous and rambunctious act endured. Ultimately, at some point during the early morning hours the noise ceased. And just then, I heard a deputy unlock the cell door and yell out, *"Roll over!"* Bewildered and perplexed, I waited to see the other guys' movements before I proceeded, for I had no idea what this meant. I watched as they slowly and methodically rolled out of their bunks, and moved to an open area of the cell, which I later learned was called the day room. This was another portion of this large cell area which contained a shower, a toilet, two tables and two phones. On the outside of the bars of the cell was a television hanging from a wall. After every man was securely fixed on this side of the cell, the deputy turned a key and a steel door slid in place locking us in the day room. One of the guys instantly turned the television on to a local news station, which didn't stupefy me at all seeing as how I've learned that inmates gravitate to the negativity of life. I kept an eye on the other inmates to ascertain what was expected of me. Some withdrew to the top of the tables, while others lay upon the cold hard concrete floor. All of them lethargically, without reservation, collapsed into a stupor. Spent, I found a spot against the wall and slumped to the floor, stuffed my arms into the sleeves of my shirt and dropped my head between bended knees. I was depleted. *Miserable* is the only way to describe this state of affairs. The local news stated that it was 4:30 A.M., and this condition seemed to have lingered for hours. Sometime during this misery, the deputies and a porter brought around breakfast trays, and slid them through an open slot in the wall. Being exasperated after what seemed to be an eternity, the steel gated door ultimately slid open, and it allowed us to journey back to the section of the cell where the beds were. All the other guys would crawl back into their beds and sleep until they brought the lunch trays around. For me this was my time of solace as I stayed on the day room side meditating and watching the local stations that I hadn't seen for years. I came to need this time because as evening drew near so did the rap videos, the cussing, the yelling, the vulgarity, and the clamorous disrespect to women and society as a whole. Never before had I heard such vulgarity used in an entire sentence! This intimated that this was the only vocabulary these men knew, and because my court date was not scheduled for three more days, I had to endure this nightly ritual. I felt like I was *literally* going to lose my mind! The noise was invariable and unending throughout each night! I swear, there were so many mornings and so many nights that I just wanted to cry! Just sob my heart out! I couldn't eat, I couldn't sleep, and I couldn't even think! The only meal I seemed to halfway be able to stomach was lunch, and that was only because I knew that soon after eating they would all hibernate back in their bunks. Even with being imprisoned, I've never known such isolation. I encountered situations while being in this twelve man cell that were deplorable, sickening, and unbearable to most human beings. The humiliation of having to cover your body with a sheet while using the toilet; this coincidentally being the same sheet you cover your body with at night. I oriented my body so that I would only use the facilities during their time of hibernation. Like tracing over bears in a cave, I methodically maneuvered around these creatures.

When my court date finally arrived on Thursday morning, I had reached a point to where I didn't care what they did with me. I just wanted out of this cell! The deputy came and transported me back to the same holding area as when I first arrived, and the stench of the morning was no different than it was during that night. A few deputies entered the room and called several names of men who were to be escorted to the courtroom area. Mine was one of them. One by one, we stood in line, waiting to be cuffed and shackled together. Like a convoy of a chain gang, we were strategically maneuvered to the passageway of the court. It was all so familiar to me as we traveled down a flight of stairs and into an elevator. These were the exact steps I journeyed six years ago upon my appearance before the Judge for my sentencing hearing. With each step that I traversed, the memory became more evident; much more real than I imagined it being so long ago. It seemed that I even remembered the dust on the steps. I felt such humiliation when I was told to face the wall after entering the elevator, as if these men, the deputies, I was once affiliated with couldn't bear to see my face. My eyes didn't leave the deputies as I noticed their neatly pressed uniforms, their weapons on their sides, and ear pieces in their ears. On seeing them, I reflected on my time of being a plain clothes officer with the Highway Patrol. The times I provided security for dignitaries such as the President of the United States, the Vice President, and the Secretary of State. And now, this day, I'm the one being guarded, yet under much different circumstances. This was a very humbling experience for me. As I watched them, they had no idea of the thoughts raging through my mind. In shame, I wanted to cry, but something deep within me wouldn't allow me to travel this concourse; this place I've journeyed so many times. Again, I wondered if these deputies escorting me knew of my past – if they knew I was once one of them. Furthermore, I wondered if they even cared.

Upon entering the courtroom, I was told by the deputy to sit next to the other inmates in the jury box. I noticed several members of my family sitting in attendance, and I was cognizant of the presence of a cousin who has been very dear to me. My heart longed for them as I gazed briefly at them. It took this constrain for my eyes to be enlightened about the goodness of my family. I believe I wanted this more so now, for them, than for myself. Sitting in the courtroom took me back six years as I remembered the endurance of an eight day trial; stress, guilt, remorse, and shame ate at the fiber of my core as news cameras marked my every move. The lasting memory I have of this courtroom is of reaching a point of not knowing who I was, or even caring. The feeling of literally dying inside, and according to my family, looking just that way as they said that I looked like a cancer patient taking my last breath. Since that time, we've talked about how far I've come and smile with astonishment at God's grace. However, during that time there was no joy in my life, and no smile could be found within me. And honestly, I didn't know if I would ever find it again.

While waiting for my name to be announced from the docket, a man who I learned was from the public defender's office unexpectedly approached me. Right then and there, my dreams and hopes were shattered. He came to where I was seated in the jury box, asked if I was Mr. McCormick, and advised me that this hearing was for a formality of misapplied wording in my transcripts. During my sentencing hearing, my transcript applied the wording that the defendant *'may be'* on post release control upon release of stated prison term. It should have stated the defendant *'will be'* on post release control." Indignant, I glared at him and angrily whispered, *"That's it! That's all I came back here for?"* At that moment, my name was called, and I stood before the Judge. He explained to me the reason for my appearance before the court was a misinterpretation of wording, though I knew I was appearing for one word! Your Honor asked if I had anything that I wanted to say, but through shear and utter disappointment, words eluded me. In undertone I could only mutter, *"No Sir."* I was devastated!

Just as I turned to leave the podium, the public defender glanced at me with a smirk on his face. To this very day, that's the closest I've ever come to wanting physically to restructure a man's appearance with no thought of stipulation. I walked out of the courtroom and couldn't bear to look back at my family. I made that mistake six years ago; I couldn't chance this venture again. I wanted this for them more so than for myself. I feel like I've let them down, and I couldn't fashion looking into their eyes. I merely turned and sauntered out of the courtroom. There is no quality of utterance to describe the anguish of my being. Never before have I endured the savor of being so depleted. Never before in my life have I been so tired. In essence; *I'm done!*

While being escorted back to the twelve man cell, I no longer looked at the deputies as I did just earlier. I looked only to the ground, for that's where my heart and spirit were. Besides, I had no strength to hold my head up, or even to mark my steps. Upon arriving to the cell, I was greeted with a bologna sandwich and a cup of juice, as if to say, *"Welcome back!"* With the steel door closing behind me, I was left to embark on my mental journey with these other eleven inmates; a journey I so desperately wanted to relinquish.

I made a valiant attempt to compress my tears as I placed a call to my mother. I didn't want her to know that during this struggle, the tears were streaming down my face. And though she gave a valiant effort for my sake, her hurt and pain permeated through her voice as I'm sure my tears did to her. I told her that I didn't understand why this wasn't it – why God did not allow this to be the open door for me. I heard the pain in her voice as she found herself once again being a source of comfort for me. While talking with her and asking about my family, I seemed to be the only one confused as she told me directly; *"Everyone says that this too is a test from the Lord."* But from my perspective, if this is of God, the reasoning behind it is difficult for me to comprehend. All I know is at the moment I'm afflicted beyond human comprehension, even more than she could ever fathom. I was *outraged*! I was furious with God, and silently, while lying in my bunk amongst all the disarray, I conveyed my grief to Him. The following morning, after the roll-over period expired, gingerly, I traipsed the cell and tacitly communed with God. I was taken aback as the hurt within me unexpectedly began to gyrate into gratefulness. I found myself uttering silent, and filled with tears of joy for what God has already done in my life, and all the while being mindful of my surroundings, and not wanting anyone to see my tears.

The next few days passed, and I hadn't yet been transported back to prison. I grew intensely wearisome because the disarray of these inmates' actions seemed to only worsen with each juncture of time. Through the midst of the chaos, I tried to read a Bible that I found laying on the cell floor. Within my inner being I silently prayed, *"Lord; if You don't hasten, I'm going to lose my mind!"* I felt that I was being bereaved of everything I knew and I plummeted to a state of lunacy. I experienced a grave disorder of my mind that seemed to impair my capacity to function amongst these people! I felt the onslaught psychologically, as I struggled daily to retain my sense of soundness. Suddenly, I found a source of stability and strength while reading Psalm 138:3. It read:

> *In the day when I cried out, you answered me, and made me bold with strength in my soul.*

In my beseeching, He provided what I needed. The entire time I was in this cell, I felt His hedge of protection encompassing me physically. Moreover now, I feel it mentally; even if just enough to sustain me for one more night.

The following day an argument ensued between three of the guys and one other inmate. He, like me, was an outsider to these guys, and didn't fit the dimension of their understanding. However, I was accepted into this sphere of theirs, and he wasn't. They rend their shirts and began to encircle him as lions do their prey. One of the guys told him, *"You'd better hit the inner-com button on the wall for the deputies' cause you getting ready to get messed up! You ain't getting no more food trays, or nothing!"* This all was taking place only a few feet away from me, yet not once did I feel physically threatened. It was as though I wasn't even there! I watched as this man stood for a few seconds, his pride seemingly contemplating his options, which from my perspective there was only one. Inwardly, I was yelling, *"Push the button you fool!"* For all intents and purposes, I wanted to walk to the wall and push it for him, when with a half-witted leisurely advance he maneuvered to the wall, and pushed the button. Upon hearing the deputies' voice, he said, *"I'm about to get jumped on by three dudes!"* Soon after he was retrieved from the cell. As the night went on, the same guy who recognized me my first night here, apparently seeing the astonishment on my face, said to me, *"They'll be here to take you back tomorrow school."* Oh, how right I hoped he was.

The following morning during roll-over, I laid on the cold hard concrete floor, and I hoped to hear the sound of keys tracing down the corridor. Suddenly, the cell door opens and the deputy said the words I'd been longing to hear. *"Pack it up McCormick!"* Ah! Never before has the broadcast of my name sounded so satisfying! The strangest thing then took place. The other inmates awoke, and one by one they shook my hand, gave me a hug, and each told me, *"Good luck school!"* It's amazing. These men *literally* put me through a living nightmare. Yet, even in the tenure of what I went through, this single moment of goodwill far outweighs it all.

The storms of life will always come; but never before in life have I been tested mentally as I was during the duration of these ten days. Lord willing, I never will be again. By virtue of this stint, I learned a life's lesson.

—◆—

While at work in the school building one afternoon, the chaplain called me into his office. He looked at me curiously, and said, *"There is something different about you."* I asked, *"What do you mean Chap?"* To which he replied, *"Since you came back from court, you seem to have a sense of peace about you; as though you have truly relinquished everything into the hands of God."* I explained how my time of affliction at the county jail elevated me to level of dependency upon God that I never knew existed. He told me about how good it was to perceive God's Glory upon me. I honestly don't know what it was that he saw within me; I know only what I felt. I was tired! Tired of fighting this battle in my mind and soul. After sustaining the experience of the county jail, I must relinquish my all to the One who controls all. Later that evening as I read my Bible, I reflected upon the events of those ten days. Like a shepherd to his flock, my heart directed me to Psalm 77:

> *I cried unto God with my voice, even unto God with my voice; and He gave ear unto me. In the day of my trouble I sought the Lord: my sore ran in the night, and ceased not: My soul refused to be comforted. I remembered God, and was troubled: I complained, and my spirit was overwhelmed. Thou holdest mine eyes waking: I am so troubled that I cannot speak. I call to remembrance my song in the night: I commune with my own heart: and my spirit made diligent search.*

Looking back through the many sleepless nights and tears I've shed; He was always there. God never left me; He was always right there clutching my every tear. So, for me to hear the chaplain say, *"It's good to see that you've given it all over to God,"* compels me to shrug my shoulders; for there is no other alternative for me. Another Psalm I read says this: *"Whither shall I go from Thy spirit? Or whither shall I flee from thy presence?"* Through the entity of my predicament, my soul is anchored in the Lord.

The following Sunday for church service we had a guest speaker whose message pierced my heart. I closed my eyes while dropping my head, not in shame, but rather in confirmation of her words. She said, *"For someone sitting in here right now, as crazy as it may sound to others, this prison experience is the best thing to ever have happen to you."* She continued, *"Just as a father does with his child, God had to put you in a timeout!"* I closed my eyes and dropped my head, and reflected back to the times of my life as a State Trooper and the occasions of me being on a collision course with life. I deliberated on the time when the chaplain spoke of my life being like a train derailment. I heard another pastor once say, *"Life has a way to shut your mouth!"* I look back and perceive just how far I have come. From being a man eroding daily in the dawning of a gray Trooper's uniform, full of pride and deceit; to a man who is now in state blues, full of humility and integrity. And oddly enough, it's the dawning of this blue outfit that has changed every part of me, and made me a better human being. I may not be all that I have the potential to be, but I'm striving. Just as this pastor said, *"This is the best thing ever to have happened in my life, to bring about change."* And thanks be to God, for I'm more than I used to be.

———◆———

Thinking about my past and all I've left behind, I find myself in situations where I'm led to share my story to more and more people. A younger inmate who has been here only a couple of months has in some way attached himself to me as I have to him. Increasingly, I've been sharing my life's story with him which has bounded our friendship. Like so many others before him, he inevitably began sharing openly the story of his life with me. He was experiencing personal issues concerning his fiancée, and inadvertently I became a source he trusted. It astounds me that with all the blunders in my life in the area of relationships, including the reason for my being here, still, I'm accounted worthy to pacify someone else's needs. These moments astonishes me.

I was working out in the gym one Sunday afternoon when I observed the C.O., who regularly works my pod, working overtime this particular day in the gym. I went to the recreation office to sign out a piece of equipment when he asked if I had a visit earlier in the day. This led to further conversation and before I knew it, I was sharing with him the chronicles of my life. I noticed he listened very intently as I shared

131

my story, and I was amazed to learn that he didn't know of my prior profession as a State Trooper. Just as shame began to rear its ugly head, unexpectedly, I became overwhelmed and found myself fighting back tears as I spoke of the love, care, and support my family has bestowed upon me. This C.O. abruptly stopped me and said, *"But by the grace of God, I could be in the same position as you McCormick. I've done many things in my lifetime that could have, and should have ended me up right in here."* He told me about how during his shift each night he observes the goings on of the pod, and how I'm esteemed differently than other inmates. He explained about how he kept an eye on me when I came back from court and perceived how I seemed to stay the course through the misfortune of not going home. He said to me, *"A lot of people would have given up after going through what you did. The first thing they would have done was throw their Bible away and say I give up! But your faith didn't waiver."* Our conversation ended with him telling me to keep doing all that I have been because one day my breakthrough is coming. I left the gym, walked around the track, and thought about how I seem to always be placed in situations and circumstances where I'm compelled to give a documentary of my past. Men flock to me sharing problems and concerns which seemingly always leads to the testament of my life. Upon my arrival here, I didn't want my identity as a State Trooper known to anyone. But now, after so many years, through some grand design, there remains no safe haven for my secret. Though my family and my love have tried to explain to me on visits, still, I have bickering within my mind toward comprehending it all. That was, until I received a card in the mail a few days later which read:

> *For God to use your painful experiences, you must be willing to share them. You have to stop covering them up, and you must admit your faults, failures, and fears. Doing this will probably be your most effective ministry. People are always more encouraged when we share how God's grace helped us in weakness, than when we brag about our strengths. God says 'yes' to who you are!*

Upon reading this card, and having several talks with my family and first love, I've come to believe that God desires a Christ – like ministry from me while being incarcerated, as well as when I'm released. And the only way to perform this is for others to see my wounds, and find healing within their own. I believe that the greatest of life's messages come from the effectiveness of your deepest hurts. In essence; the things I've been most embarrassed, ashamed, and reluctant to share, are the very tools God wants to expose to touch others' lives.

I sat in my bunk one afternoon during count time watching a popular television talk show. The story was about a well-known female Olympic track star, who went to prison after her confession of using performance enhancing drugs. Tears whelped in my eyes as she accounted about losing everything. The respect of the world, the shame, hurt, and anguish she brought to her family, especially her mother and children. Her story pricked my heart, as well as her constrain in her voice, because it was once my own. I thought, that here's a woman who seemingly had it all! Albeit through one mistake; through one bad choice, utterly lost everything meaningful in her life. She spoke of meeting other women while incarcerated, who like her, are paying the ultimate price for poor choices in life. Through her heartwarming devotion, I understood clearly that misfortune can truly strike at anyone's front door. Although she spoke of her loss, she spoke just as much about all that she had gained through this affliction. She attained a sense of self-worth, respect, and integrity that only she could fathom by her intimacy of imprisonment. I have a familiarity of this same intimacy. I thought about my moment with the parole board as she described the freeing of her inner self from the guilt and condemnation of the lie she was living. Her tears flowing; implicitly I stood watching with my own. With the comfort and support of this woman's story, I've come to understand that I don't have to seek the approval of everyone. Admittedly or not, we've all made mistakes in life. Mine, like hers, just happened to have cost me more than others. Like her; it cost me everything. The tears and the pain at times are unbearable, but I know God has a plan, and I'm committed to it. That commitment frees me from worry. It's freed me from guilt, and condemnation. Just as she experienced, there was no greater feeling of release than when I came clean with the truth of my incident. Feeling as pure in my heart as a child, there are no words to describe self- respect.

I've had to endure so much pain. The loss of my father, both of my grandmothers, and most recent, the heaviness of my first love going away to Africa. Yet, even with a broken heart, I *still* have the strength to stand.

MY FIRST LOVE

As the day came of our last visit together, my heart hurt in places I never knew existed. The night before, all I could do was hurt. I was hurting to the very depth of my soul and the core of my being. She had just visited the day before, and as always, it was beautiful, just as she was beautiful. *Oh!* How I loved her; how I was going to miss her. I was going to miss every part of her beyond measure. She's become the very air I breathe and I cannot imagine not seeing her for a whole year. I can't imagine not feeling her touch; I can't imagine not breathing, for an entire year, for she simply takes my breath away.

As this Sunday morning arrived, I went to a window in the pod which faces the parking lot, and watched her as she arrived. I stood in the window and just watched her. I watched as she walked across the parking lot, remembering every single movement of her. I didn't want to miss one single thing about her – about this last visit. I wanted to memorize every single part of her. As the C.O. called my name, I walked slowly to the visiting room taking the long way around. I needed time to gather myself. This was a pain unlike anything I've ever known. I walked in and saw her beautiful face, and my heart did as it always does, as it always has; it *melted*. We embraced, and I didn't want to let go, as I could again feel her heart beat against my chest. *Oh* how she got to me! She felt so good in my arms, and I didn't want to let her go. Not now – not ever.

Several times during our visit I tried to hold back tears, but I lost that battle. She was every part of me. I just wanted to crawl inside of her and lose myself. I feel so lost without her.

Together, we cried, we laughed, and we loved. We both knew what was coming, as the minutes and hours ticked away; even still, we held each other – without physically holding each other. This is how we were, and this is who we've become. *One*, in every way possible to be, we were one. We completed each other in every sense of the word. That's why we both hurt so bad this day, because we not only felt our own pain but even more, that of the other. It was deep, it was hard, and we could feel every part of it. Every part of each other. To see her cry tore me apart. I wanted to lean forward and kiss each tear drop from her face, tasting them with my lips. That way too, I'd have her with me. I wanted every part of her. We prayed together, and I felt the softness of her hands in mine. I then realized that this would be the last time I would feel them until she returned from Egypt. Suddenly, just when I didn't think it was possible, I fell deeper in love with her, right at that very moment. It was also at this moment that I knew I wanted to be in her every moment.

Then it happened; the C.O. yelled three words that never seemed louder the whole time I've been here. *"Visiting is over!"* I looked directly into her eyes and her tears filled my heart. I held her, pulled her close into me, and put my hand in her hair. I smelled her as I kissed her neck and her lips. I wiped tears from her eyes as I fought to hold back my own. I felt I had to, or she wouldn't be able to leave. I wouldn't be able to let her. It hurt me so deeply to watch her walk away from me; to see her standing in the doorway with tears streaming down her face. This prison time included, the hardest thing I've ever had to do was to watch her walk out that door. I so badly wanted to run and grab her, and tell her to come back. *"Please baby,"* come back to me! *Please* don't leave me! Please my love, don't go...please stay.

I sadly and quickly went back to the pod. The same window in which I watched her come, I was now watching her go. I watched, as she slowly walked with another woman across the parking lot. I saw as they embraced and she then walked to her car. It was as though I could see her tears from where I stood; certainly, I could feel them. I could taste them. Every one of them, for they were my own. She arrived at her car door, and I saw her look towards the window where I stood, as though she was looking at me one last time. She sat in her car for a while before moving, and my heart, soul, body, and spirit sat there with her. She owned every part of me, and she was taking that every part with her that day. I was so empty inside. All that day and the nights to follow, I cried rivers of tears. When I took a shower, I didn't need the water from the spicket; my tears were enough. I showered in them. What I wouldn't do to go back to that moment of praying together – of her holding my hands. Nothing can satisfy me other than her touch. Oh how I miss her so much!

⟫◆⟪

As the next few weeks passed, *oh* how I've missed her so much. My life has seemed so empty and meaningless without her. Since she's been in Egypt, I've not been able to talk with her. The mail system there is set up to where all of her mail goes through the Embassy, which doesn't run on a regular schedule. So when I receive it, it's always weeks behind. But even with that, it's just hearing from her and seeing her words on paper that makes my heart melt. Each time I open the envelope and bring the paper to my face, I hope to catch the smell of her, or just a scent of her presence. To know her hands were there, on this paper, is as if she is holding my hands as I read each letter. That's how close I feel to her; to each word she writes. I don't have the capability not to think of her. She's in every thought I have, and in everything I do. If I can't be anywhere else in this world, I'd want to be right where she is; or at least for this moment, right where her letters make me feel. I simply don't want to be anywhere else. *Ever!* I received a card from her one day that spoke everything I've ever wanted and needed to hear from anyone in my life. Words I've seemed to long desire, yet never have obtained. She found them, in one Hallmark moment:

> *You and I are connected in a way that goes beyond romance, beyond friendship, beyond what we've ever had before. It has defied time, distance, and changes in ourselves and in our lives. And it has defied every explanation except one: purely and simply, we're soul mates. I can't explain it. I just*

137

feel it. It's there in the way my spirit subtly lifts whenever we talk, how the sound of your voice brings me home in a way I can't explain. It's in the delight I feel when we laugh at exactly the same things. When I'm with you, it's like a tiny part of the universe shifts into the place it's supposed to be, and all is right with the world. These things and so many more, have made me understand that this is a once-in-a-lifetime, forever connection that could only exist between you and me. And deep in my soul, I know that our relationship is a rare gift, one that will bring us an extraordinary happiness all through our lives.

Before her leaving to go to Africa, she had told me about a special card she had saved for many months. This is the card. She told me she knew this was the card that truly speaks *us,* and she wanted to wait to send it, just before she boarded the plane to Egypt. A week or so later, I received another card from her and the words again sent my heart to depths it's never been before. There simply is no depth to measure my love for her. It transcends time or space.

If I could have only one dream come true, I'd want to spend the rest of my life with you. If I could have only one voice to hear, one smile to see, one hand to hold...I'd want yours. In a world crowded with people, there's a comfort only your caring can provide, a quiet calm at the center of things only you can give. There's a deep and abiding happiness my heart never knew till I found you (again). If I could make a difference in one life, I'd want it to be yours. I want to return all the little kindnesses you share with me day by day. I want to make your life easier when it's hard and calmer when it's chaotic. I want to be the one who treats your heart as gently and lovingly as you treat mine. I want to be everything you are to me...because the best things in my life come from having you to love.

Little does she know, next to God, she makes all the difference in my life. She's made all the difference in me. *Purely* and *simply*, she is my soul mate. The love of my life. I've never known anything like her, nor anything like *this*. And I know that I never will again. She is the best thing in my life.

One night, after working out, I was in the shower when the strongest urge came over me to call her. It was the strangest, yet most powerful feeling within my heart. It was as though a voice within my inner self-willed me towards her voice. After getting out of the shower, I went to the phone with an expectancy to hear the usual computerized voice telling me there was a block on this number. I was completely mystified when I dialed her number in Egypt and was able to get through.

Pure ecstasy filled my heart as I heard her sweet soft voice speak to me from so many miles away. We laughed almost hysterically at the pure admiration of hearing each other's voice. It seemed as though it had been so long, and wonderment took over my soul completely as we seemed to have talked for hours. *Oh!* How I've thirsted for her voice! Once more, just as so long ago, I fell in love all over again, like it was the first time. We've talked every night since, and it seems no matter the time or distance, our love and admiration for each other has only grown. I've come to discover a complete denial of myself in putting her every need, desire, and concern before my own. There is such a deep satisfaction between us that has no depth of measurement. It's simply never ending. The anguish from missing her led me to think of a verse of scripture in Psalm 69:20 which reads:

> *Reproach has broken my heart, and I am full of heaviness;*
> *I looked for someone to take pity, but there was none; and*
> *for comforters, but I found none.*

She has become all the comfort I need. In her – with her, I find solace. We take commiseration and compassion for each other and carry such heaviness in our hearts due to our distance. I can't imagine a life without her now. For me, that life doesn't exist.

She told me about a letter she'd written that was different from any I'd received; one she said that should have been written long ago. I received it, and my heart melted to my very core as her words got to me in ways so unimaginable. Since my childhood, I've been entranced with this woman, and this letter personifies why.

Lukie,

To the love of my life...you have a secret admirer in me. I am writing you this love letter as your "secret admirer" - I hope you remember me (smile). I am the one who has loved you your entire life. We've known each other since childhood and that has been some time ago. Although it's been some 30 plus years since we have seen each other, I have to tell you a secret...I've never stopped loving you.

As adults, when we look back on our childhood, a lot of times we ask ourselves "What was I thinking? Oh! If I had only done this or that." Well, when I look back and think of us, I don't have a lot of memories...I have a lot of <u>feelings</u>. I feel that when we were together, that our hearts were one (even as kids). I <u>felt</u> the biggest pain when I hurt you. I don't remember how, I just know I did. But I also remember being hurt; I believe it was retaliation and saving face with the guys (smile). However, no matter what the situation was or the reason, I do remember looking into your eyes and <u>feeling</u> you.

As we grew older and experienced a lot of life lessons, you <u>never</u>, <u>never</u> left my heart. I always wondered "What is he doing...How is he doing...Is he happy?" <u>Never</u> in my wildest dreams would I have thought that the love I once knew as a child ran this deep. A depth that has no boundaries. A love like no other...because it is God given.

This letter may seem a little weird and I apologize – but let me explain. This is a "love letter." Over a year ago, you should have received this letter instead of the card... "A voice from your past." I felt then, as I do now, I just didn't have the courage to write it down. I didn't know how you felt and my heart could not withstand any rejection from you...anyone else – yes...you – no. I realize now that you could never reject your own heart, because it's been yours since before we were born. I truly believe our hearts beat as one...that God made me from your bone...and that we will love each other till the end of time (and thereafter). I am yours Lukie. On February 9th, we found Church St. again. We found "Home." I Love you.

She enthralls me beyond belief. She has an irresistible power over me that holds me totally spellbound. I often wonder how and why we ever left each other from so long ago. In the purest form and sense of the word, she's *beautiful!* I'm left only to thank God for this awesome wonder that He's once again brought into my life; from so long ago.

REMOVING SELF TO HELP OTHERS

One Tuesday afternoon I was working in my classroom when the Chaplain came and asked me to come to his office when I had a chance. I thought he had something he wanted to talk with me about regarding myself or my family, but I could see on his face that he was very troubled within himself. His heart and spirit seemed to be really heavy. As I entered his office and closed the door, he looked to have tears in his eyes as he began to ask how I was doing...though I could sense his question was a formality to what was really troubling him

He began to talk with me about the Chaplain who used to be here, but left for another institution. He's been stricken with some type of serious disease that's brought a lot of hardship on himself and his family. As he spoke with me I could see the pain in his face and the hurt in his voice. He talked of how short life is and we should cherish every moment we have. He seemed to have such a heavy heart, and I couldn't help but wonder what was truly going on within him. Why would he want to talk with me about issues of his heart; with an inmate, scared by life himself? But something within me told me to just listen; just sit and listen to his voice, his hurt and his pain. The more I sat and listened, I realized it wasn't about me at all, rather about him just needing someone he was familiar with, and that he could trust with the cares of his heart.

At least for this moment, I was there and I listened. He didn't need me to say a word. It was as though his heart was saying, *"Please, just hear me out. I need someone to talk to"*. As he finished pouring out his heart about other personal issues concerning him, he quietly looked me in the eye, laid his bead back against his chair, and simply said, *"Thank you for your time"*. As I left his office, I could feel my heart being overcome with compassion. Part of me wanted to cry, yet there was a part of me that was comforted as well. Being able to be there for someone of his position brought a sense of calming to my spirit. The fact that he trusted me with his inner most hurts gave me a sense of *being* within these prison walls.

At least for these few moments of time, I wasn't viewed as an inmate, but as someone trustworthy, empathetic enough to be given one's pains within my hands; and entrusted enough to keep them there.

A few days later, this all was confirmed to me another staff member. I had just came in from working out an taking a shower when the pod C.O. came to my cell and told me the C.O. working the connecting cadre pod wanted to see me. This is the same C.O. who frequently talks with me about the Lord. As he and I talked, he told me that God is going to use me in a mighty way. He said that I will be able to help so many through my testimony because I'm not afraid to share my heart. He said he believes that I'll help a lot of people, especially those who are afraid to love again, as I was. He told me that through my experience, I'll help many hurting hearts and souls.

As I left from speaking with this C.O., I couldn't help but think of the favor of God. The fact that members of the staff talk with me so openly and honestly is unheard of, none the less frowned upon by both staff and inmates. I thought of the Chaplain and wondered if this C.O. was right. Did my being there for him in his time of need in any way truly help him? I have to wonder, *"Is my time in prison meant for some greater good?"* My greatest failures may have been bad, but in that, I'm led to think of Joseph when he talks with his brothers:

> *Fear not: for am I in the place of God? But as for you, ye thought evil against me: but God meant it unto good, to bring to pass, as it is this day, to save much people alive.*

143

So in this time of imprisonment, I can only hope that all that's been wrong and gone wrong in and throughout my life, that there is something that can be turned into good. If not for myself, then certainly for someone else.

—◇—

As another holiday season draws near, my heart too, draws closer to loneliness. Christmas has always been my most favorite time of year, and this one takes on an even more special meaning for me. I think of her being in Egypt, and what it would feel like, be like, to be with her on Christmas day. I realize that this is part of the punishment of being in prison; being away from family and home. And now, away from her.

I began to receive several Christmas cards, but there were two that really touched me more than others. One being from my mother – and the words were simple and few, yet so powerful and touching. It read:

> *Son, I wonder if you know how often I whisper in my heart, God keep him safe, I love him so.*

As I read those words, I had to close my cell door, as I couldn't stop the tears rolling down my face. Here I am, a grown man in prison, yet at that moment, I felt like a little child in need of his mother's touch. Even on visits, my mother has a way to get to my heart like no one else, just with a look. With a mother to her only son; she simply has a way.

The other touching card was from a friend of mine here who has cancer. I came in from work one day and found this card on my bed just before count time. It was as though he placed it there at a time when he knew I wouldn't be able to respond right away. It read:

> *"I know this is no ordinary Christmas card, but this hasn't been no ordinary year for either of us. With that said, I just want to thank you my friend, that in light of all that was going on in your life, you made sacrifices to nurture me, both physically and spiritually. Well my brother, I just wanted you to know your efforts didn't go un-noticed,*

and they were greatly appreciated! Thank you Luke, for everything; but most of all, thank you for your friendship, for it's what I value most! Merry Christmas my friend!"

When I saw him later that evening as we went to work-out, no words had to be spoken. I simply gave him a head nod, and he returned the same to me. I believe if any words would have passed, the wall of our prison manhood would have been torn down like the wall of Jericho. He and I have been close for many years. We knew what the other was thinking at that very moment, and that was enough.

A few days later the Chaplain again called me into his office. He said to me, *"I want to commend you. Even though your situation is frustrating, being away from your family these many years and Christmas', and now also this young lady coming back into your life; ever since you came back from court, you've seemed to be stronger and more content. You've moved yourself out of the way, gave it all over to God, and know you had to do what's necessary to make it through this."* He told me that I may not always show it on my face, or even feel it in my heart, but in my spirit, it shows. He again said, *"I commend you for going through all that you have, and standing the way that you are."* I thanked him as I walked out of his office but little did he know my heart is broken. I'm so empty inside.

Later this same afternoon as I walked back to the pod, I looked into the sky and noticed the beautiful formation of the clouds. They looked like pillars of mountains and I couldn't help but wonder if they looked the same outside this prison fence. Though the realization is that they do, still, I couldn't help but wonder. I also couldn't help but wonder what Christmas looked like outside this fence. I wonder what everything looks like outside of here. This time that I've been away leaves me to feel so out of touch. The thought of being away from home another Christmas brings tears to my eyes. No matter the number of years I've spent away from home, it doesn't get any easier. Sometimes, I feel like telling God, *"I'll cry till you tell me to let it go and let it be. For it's Your will, Lord, that's best for me!"* And with that – I'll spend another Christmas with my tears falling like snowflakes and wish I could somehow drift in the pillar of these clouds.

One Saturday morning an inmate asked me about whether I was receiving a visit or not I told him due to the weather being bad that I wasn't getting one until Sunday. He jokingly said, *"Good, you can spend the day with us, then!"* I laughed and told him, *"I've spent the day with you for the past seven years."* His response then took me aback. He looked at me with the most serious face and asked, *"How many souls have you saved since you've been here?"* Then quickly, before I could say a word, he responded with, *"You saved mine. Think about it. That may be the reason why you're here!"* With that, he turned and walked away.

I was left standing with my thoughts. I literally stood there on the range and watched him walk to his cell. I thought of the many inmates I've spoken to, not only about the Lord, but about life in general. I couldn't help but wonder if in some way I had an influence on them or on their lives. I thought back to a message a guest speaker spoke one Sunday during church service. *"You didn't get arrested, you got rescued."* Maybe this inmate was right. Maybe God had to lay me down, so I could look up, and in doing that, He gave me the humbleness to be a help or blessing to someone else. It seems as though my time in prison has not only been about myself and the changes made within me, but also for the needs of others. It's not only been done to me, but also through me.

<hr>

A few days later I watched the Inauguration of the new President, and it was one of the proudest, yet hardest things I've ever watched. On a personal note, I've never been more proud to see the heights our country reached on this day. However, on a professional level, it saddened me to watch the many Secret Service Agents provide protection and security for the many dignitaries there. I saw myself in so many aspects, and it deeply saddened me. All I could think about was the mistake I made, and how I'll never see that part of life again. The part that I miss more than any other area or aspect of the job I once had as a State Trooper. Watching the events of this day agonized and haunted me within my soul. I began to point out the agents in the crowd, one after the other. The suits, the looks, the stern glares of awareness. I miss it all.

As I saw the military personnel, I thought of her. I wondered what it would be like to stand by her side so proud of her. I knew she would understand how I felt. Then a feeling of deflation came over me as I learned Ohio sent several plain clothes State Troopers to the Inauguration to help provide security. My heart was torn apart as emptiness set within me. *"It could have been me."* I couldn't help but know that it would've been me. I could have been counted and called in the number of those providing security for the most honorable event in America. Yet, due to my mistake, I'm left out. And now, my name and number is called for something else. I'm left to wonder, *"Did I get arrested from the Ohio State Patrol, to play a part in rescuing someone else?"* As I spoke this hurt within me to a friend, he tried to give my soul consolation with some encouraging words. *"There are much greater things out there for you to do. When one door closes, another one opens!"* As I watched the many officers and agents, in suits and ties and overcoats – I pray, good Lord, how I pray that I can turn that door handle soon. For the most hurtful part of it all is that I know there will always be a place in my heart for this. Though it didn't show on my face, the tears were running within my heart.

LOVING GIFTS

One brisk Wednesday evening my workout partner and I decided to workout outside. We caught a day that the temperature was about 40 degrees. During a break between sets, I happened to notice how crystal clear and awe inspiring the sky was, and at that moment I saw a single star alone in the sky. My mind instantly raced to her, as I imagined in my heart that this star was her gazing over me from Egypt. My gaze was transfixed on this lonely star because I feared that the removal of my sight from this beam from Heaven would equate to closing my eyes to the presence of my love. Taking my eyes off of it was as taking my eyes off of her. Her beautiful face filled my view, and I was incapable of arresting my gaze. I was entranced. I didn't want to stop looking at her – looking at me. It made me think of my mother telling me one day on a visit how she always calls to see if anyone has come to visit me, because she worries about me being alone. This star also made me think of how it's going to be the first time we're together. Just sitting face to face and gazing into each other's eyes so deeply, as if looking straight into the other's soul. The deepness, the warmth, the passion – Uh! She *so* gets to me! She is such a part of my very being. This time apart has been the hardest thing I've had to endure. It's as if God is using it as a testament to my prior being – to change everything about whom I once was. He's bestowed in me a passion and yearning for her unlike anything I've ever experienced or known. I'm being taught the true meaning and feeling of love, in every facet of the word. To crave her in ways so unimaginable is being engraved deep within my soul. It's as though He's saying, *"I'm going to see if you're serious this time."* Because

God knows, I've had many failed relationships in my lifetime. I've spent many years throughout my life searching for something meaningful and true. I've had many females in my life, but never before have I had a woman that means the world to me. It's amazing that just a simple glimpse of a star could draw me so close to her.

She is my Heaven on earth; my gift from God. I want to be intimate with every aspect of her being, so passionately, and for our eyes to study every inch of each other. Being away from her has made me to know and realize that she is a treasure which I long to explore.

And just like this star, I cannot wait for her eyes to be looking upon me and my very being.

———————

One Saturday during a visit, my mother, sister and I were discussing events of my past which led to my incarceration. They both shared some things with me that I wasn't aware of, and quite frankly, it surprised me. My mother told me, that to this day, a lot of people believe there is more to the story about what happened that night than what's known. She said that people believe that I walked in on my wife while she was with another man, and that I've somehow repressed this memory out of my mind. She also said that anyone who knows me knows that I acted out of character.

It amazes me that after all of these years, people still have a mysterious fascination about the actual events of that fateful evening. What's even more astonishing is the level of support and understanding I receive from so many. My mom spoke about the clemency hearing which occurred about three and a half to four years ago, and how members of the parole board displayed a sense of compassion and understanding for my situation. All I know is that once I confessed my identity before the parole board, my life and who I was began to change. My only memory from that day is when I was asked *"Was this an accident?"* From that moment on, it was as though God was whispering in my heart, *"Now, just trust Me. Allow Me to make the necessary changes in your life."*

My life has made me to ponder the story of Jacob. Once he confessed to the Angel of God who he was, the first thing God did was change his name. Like Jacob, once I confessed my wrong, and in that, who I was, my identity at that moment was changed. The moment I was faced with that question, I could no, longer run from my failures. God saw my weaknesses, and deep down I knew them too. He peered into my soul, and my flaws emerged from the darkness into my awareness. And just as He did with Jacob, God had to touch a stubborn part of me to slow me down, and show me He's in control. Jacob's transformation was in his character; my restoration had to occur within my relationships... and in that, a change within my heart. My strength – what I've always tried to control is my heart. Now it too, belongs to God.

———◆———

I contemplate about the events of my life over the past year, how God brought my childhood sweetheart back into my life. My heart and my identity, He's placed in her hands. Like Jacob's thigh, God put a limp in my heart, to remind me that for the rest of my life, my trust is to be in Him and Him alone.

I received a letter from her one day telling me her feelings about our first year anniversary. She said to me: *"It was the day that I was made whole. It was confirmation that I never stopped loving you. Where you are was no matter to me, but who you are is everything."* He has made her my reminder. She, my heart, is one thing I'll never run from again. What she doesn't know, and what I conceal from her, is that every correspondence yields a torrent of tears. And with every tear, I yearn even more to be in her presence.

So maybe what my mother said was true and maybe there was something more to what happened that night. My soul was in the initial phase of being refurbished. I was blind to God's transformative touch, because I was rendered sightless by the emotional filth in my heart. It kept me from seeing myself.

One Saturday morning, a C.O. called me for a visit, and something within me told me today was going to be something different; something special. As I walked into the visiting room and checked in with the officer at the desk, I noticed my mother and baby sister sitting there; however, though I could not see who, there appeared to be someone sitting with them. As I approached where they were, my oldest daughter leaned forward from behind them, and almost instantly my heart melted. We embraced and I said to her, *"I've missed you so much!"* She whispered in my ear the same. In holding her, I couldn't the overwhelming feeling brewing within me, and tears began to slowly run down my face. I tried not to look at her, so as to hide my emotions, but then I made the mistake of looking over at my mother. And just as the day I learned of my love going to Egypt, my mother once again shed tears for me and with me. For the first time in many years, since the night I had to hold and comfort her on the porch of her mother's house during my trial to assure her I was okay, my daughter watched as her daddy cried. Only this time, they were tears of joy and not sadness.

Several times during the visit, my mother and sister watched my daughter and me, and they just smiled at the way we laughed and shared. At one point I heard them whisper to each other, *"Aren't they cute?"* They left early so that she and I could have time together, and we enjoyed each other so much. We discussed things openly; more openly than I ever imagined. She told me about her boyfriend and their relationship, as I told her about my new found love that returned to my life, telling of how she was my very first girlfriend. I explained to her that I had wanted to speak with her about it for a while, but was apprehensive due to not wanting to appear disrespectful with regard to her mother. I wasn't seeking her approval, I just wanted for her to know. I explained to her how for me, no one in my life has been important enough to talk about with her. Though it sounds beyond the realm of reason, which includes my second wife. For me, this time, it means everything, and I wanted for her to know. I wanted her to hear about it from me. She looked at me with a huge smile on her face and said, *"Daddy, I'm happy for you. All of that stuff with my mom was so many years ago."* When I looked into her eyes, it brought such warmth to my heart. It was as though I was looking into a mirror. There were times that we'd say nothing, but just gaze at each other with a deepness that only a father and daughter could understand. It was as though we were seeing silently within ourselves at how much the other has grown throughout the years. As I'm seeing my beautiful daughter grow into a mature young lady, she is also seeing me grow not only as a man, but also as her dad. She knows about the things I've been through in my life, and she now sees the things that I've overcome. Without a word being spoken, she could see what only a daughter who knows her father could, and that was an effervescence of resilience. I would like to believe that's what brought the silent smiles within her.

One morning, before beginning my job at the school, I talked with a teacher that I've become very fond of. He and I have talked on several occasions, and he's become someone I confide in about personal issues in my life. I wanted to show him a picture that I had received of my love and her mother. In speaking about her, I could feel the tears secretly and silently begin to rise within my eyes and heart. It always seems that whenever he and I talk about her, I find myself only able to go to a certain point for the fear of him seeing me cry. I don't know what it is about our conversations, or the things he says to me, but the effect always resonates deep within. I really admire this man and his perspective on things and on life in general. As we talked, I shared with him how excruciating it is to be away from her. To literally have my every moment consumed by thoughts of her. I told him about how we talk on the phone at set times every day, and how those are the moments that fuel my existence. I live every single second of every single day – striving to embrace those *moments,* because those are the only moments when my pain subsides. I just long to hear her breathe. In sharing her Egyptian experience, it confounds me that an exotic, provocative, and exciting location like Egypt is not the same for her in my absence. Even though each day in prison is as bland as the next, it is inexplicable to me that she wants to hear about it. To share with her – me. I bear the hours and minutes of this time of incarceration, enchanted with thoughts of our union. It seems to be all that I live for. It's certainly all that matters.

He recounted the anguish, despair, and loneliness he endured while studying in Switzerland apart from his wife. He explained that the pinnacle of each day was a telephone rendezvous at 1:00 am, and how all of life pointed to that moment. The early morning meetings just weren't enough emotional sustenance to carry him through the day. He spoke about a tour of the Swiss Alps, and all the beauty and majesty and how strange it was to be summer at the bottom of the mountain and winter at the top. But the snowcapped covered beauty of the grand mountain scenery did not fill the empty and hollow feeling that endured while separated from his wife. When he reached the top, all else paled, because she wasn't there with him. It made me think about how in life you can reach the milestones you've always dreamed of, but without that *special someone* there to share it with you, the luster is lost. He experienced the beauty, wonder, and splendor of God's creation, yet his only thought was of her. Her absence dampened the experience like a cold rain in April. He explained that you ache for that person so much that you can't focus on everyday tasks. Throughout his days and nights there, 1:00 am is all that mattered.

A few days later I received a card that reminded me of our conversation that day. It again reminds me of how it seems that where my heart is, there hers is as well. It read:

> *All I want is to love you for the rest of my life...to wake up every morning with you by my side, knowing that no matter what happens; I'll be able to come "home" to your loving arms. All I want is to share everything with you...to talk to you about our ideas, our dreams, the little everyday things that make us laugh, and the not-so-little things that we can't help worrying about. All I want is to give you my love...as a place you can always come to for acceptance or the simple comfort that silence brings when things left unspoken can still be understood. All I want is to grow old with you...to watch our life unfold, our dreams, one by one, come true. All I want is to love you forever. All I want is you.*

I hunger and thirst for her so profoundly. All I think about and all I want is to be with her. The teacher's experience is my experience. I feel the same emotions within me. I'd give anything to feel her touch, and to hear her voice, just one more time each day. I'd solely, give anything.

———◆◆◆———

I enrolled in a program called *Soul Searching*. This program is designed for inmates to get in touch with their emotions, which for the biggest part of the population here is a very touchy area. Since being incarcerated, I've learned that men have a very difficult time with self- examination. A lot of people don't want to look in the mirror of their hearts for the fear of what they may see. It's what causes them to change. I too, had that fear. However, in the process of bringing about a change in me, it's the exact thing that once brought me to my knees in brokenness and humbleness. During this time of incarceration, I've had the opportunity that many in life never get – and that's the chance to slow down and evaluate myself. I was afraid to face the truth about myself for fear of what I would discover, so I hid behind my deceptions. But the same fear that haunted me for so long and kept me from changing is what drove me to change. Though this experience has been excruciating, through it, I chose to come out different.

In this class, men are faced with questions about the events of their past which may have directly or indirectly led them to where they are now. As one inmate was speaking, I could only anguish about the many lives I touched and hurt for being here. He spoke about the regret and distress he felt for his loved ones by putting them through this. He commented about the granddaughter he's never met, and her name he doesn't even know. He spoke about missed opportunities to see his son on the football field, in a sense, watching his own dreams shattered. I thought about the agonizing pain, guilt, and torment I experienced daily because of what I've put my mother and children through. The hurt I suffer from deep within when I walk in the visiting room and see my mother sitting there with a smile on her face for her son. Knowing that I put her here in this room, tares at me to the very core of my being.

When I'm not there for my daughter as she excels on the track and field in college, and she not being able to look in the stands and see her daddy gleaming with pride. Also, my absence at the finish line as she crossed, as I was in the past. I did this. I did it not only to myself – but more so, I did this to them, and that is a hurt within me that at times is too much to bear.

The instructor of this class one day asked if we thought our punishment fit our crimes. All I could think about was my family. My time and my crime is being away from them. To know that the one mistake I made - the one bad choice, it cost me not only my career, but it cost me everything. My soul search began well before participation in this program. Mine began the night I pulled that trigger. The night that not only changed my life forever, but the lives of my loved ones as well. I've heard some inmates say they feel as though they've been buried alive here. I choose to think of it as being planted. It's all about how I sprout and grow from this experience. As I water and feed the seed of tribulation in my heart, it has fascinated me to see the way I've flourished and become strengthened through adversity. Time is one thing that I can never get back, but it's also one thing I hope will heal the wounds, scars, and brokenness of hearts touched by me. I can only hope and pray that through my brokenness and change, it can act as a buffer or bandage to their wounds. I choose to come out of this as a better father, son, and potential husband. But more than anything, I choose to be a better man.

——◇◆◇——

One day after speaking with my love, she learned of an uncle, who is very close and dear to her heart that passed away. Therefore, she needed to come home to be with her family during this time of bereavement. For me this was a bitter sweet feeling, for I longed so desperately to see her, yet not under these circumstances. I felt helpless as I spent days and moments trying to comfort her heart, as I could feel her immense hurt and the depth of her sorrow. How I wished I could hold her and comfort her. We share and feel with such *simplicity* and *beauty* that we seem more aware of the other than of ourselves. This time; this moment, I was so aware of her and what she needed from me. Though it hurt so deeply that I'm not able to be physically present, yet I realize what she needs from me now in my absence is my ear and my heart; and for her, to allow her heart to just lay within me, as I caress the anguish lying within her. Through her tears, I felt those of my own, for God has truly made us one. Sometimes I get so tired of crying, but I've learned to never discount the wonder of my tears because they can be healing waters and the best words the heart can ever speak. This is what I wish for her today, that her heart be able to speak and release all that lies within her. I only wish I were there to catch every word spoken.

When I saw her for the first time in six months, it was as though I was seeing her for the first time all over again. *Ah!* She was so breathtakingly stunning! Nothing matches the beauty of seeing her, this woman who has changed the melody of my life. This melody, I long to play for her. Though I was unaware, I have secretly loved this woman my entire life, and nothing has made me lonelier than this secret.

As I walked into the visiting room and saw her, I engulfed her in my arms and didn't want to let go. I was so *entrenched* with her! I was taken by her scent as she emanated an air of serenity. As she spoke, her voice reached a depth within me that has never been delved into. If a rainbow makes a sound, or a flower as it grows, that would be the voice illuminating from her. I could only watch her lips as she spoke; as each word from her hung in the balance of my ears and heart.

I was able to spend the next three weekends with her, and with each day, it was like reliving the 9th of February. Everything was as she is, simply *beautiful.* The looks, the conversations, touching and feeling of her love. It all was Heavenly, and I didn't want for it to end. Each day, each moment with her was like being in the presence of an angel. She simply takes my breath away.

As the last day of our visit arrived before she had to return to Egypt, it too was like the first time she left to go there. The pain and anguish in my heart was just as strong as it was then. It was only alleviated with time. I watched again as she pulled out of the institution parking lot, and as her car made that final turn onto the roadway, it felt as though my soul was once again leaving me. I've come to realize that the pain from missing her is something that will never subside. I'm never more alone than when I'm alone without her. The only remedy is being with her for the rest of my life.

———◆———

One night, about 3:00 am, I was having a very difficult time sleeping. I sat up in my bunk, turned my night lamp on, and began to read my Bible, until I felt my eyes once again becoming heavy. As I laid down and drifted back to sleep, I had a dream about events of my past. In this dream, I was in my Highway Patrol car sitting in the driver's seat, though the amazing thing was; I had no control of the steering wheel. I passively sat and watched as my car ever so slowly spun out of control. I was paralyzed and could only observe as the car came razor close to homes, and fences in its path, and each time it approached impact with something, it gently and methodically swerved to miss. The car then spun slowly backwards, and was headed directly for a crater in the middle of the road which had construction barricades and cones blocking it. Again, as the car approached, it avoided this obstacle. As I somberly sat in the driver's seat, still observing, my hands seemingly glued to my sides, the patrol car started down the road backwards. In desperation I tried to brake, so much so that I was awakened by jamming my foot against the end of my bunk. Startled, I sat up quickly, thinking that this was so very real and too, worried that I woke my bunkie by slamming my foot against the bunk. As I tried to settle back into a slumber, my mind began to wonder about the message this dream had for me. The first and only thing that came instantly to my mind was the fact that I did not have control of the steering wheel, and it was God showing me that He has been in control of my entire life. I know within myself, that the time I was with the State Highway Patrol was the time when my life truly began to spiral downward; like the car in my dream. I concluded that avoiding the numerous obstacles was God's protective hand providing shelter from injurious life events that could have happened.

I shared this dream with the teacher at the school, whom I truly admire and trust and he felt the car represented my life journey. And though I was spinning out of control, the car was not damaged, and that shows that I was intact psychologically and spiritually. There is *still* more within my life, and there are still many miles left to travel on my life journey. I'm astonished that a career that I once held so dear would be the source of shame and derision that would cripple me to my knees. For me, my stay in prison and the interactions with the staff is a debilitating reminder of what I was, and what I did. Every time I see a corrections officer, or chat with a staff member, painful memories bombard me. I remember, and I'm ashamed and broken all over again, because I allowed myself to be where I am. But the silver lining throughout this entire experience is that I've been permeated by the loving grace of the Master of the universe. My life – my very soul, has been redeemed.

The following morning, during my daily toil, my boss and I had a conversation. Out of nowhere, he said to me, *"Two of your greatest attributes are honesty and trust. People trust you Luke, and I'm not just talking about inmates."* I was puzzled as to the origin of this conversation, because he is a very eccentric person (to say the least.) But then, I was asked by another teacher to pick up some books from another building and was astonished by a conversation with another staff member. As our paths intersected on my way to this building, this C.O. said to me, *"People have been talking about you. They say how quiet, reserved, and laid back you are. People around here really like you McCormick, and think you are a good guy."* This comment too seemed to have come from nowhere, but as I pondered it, I came to relate it to my dream, my life, and the fact or reasoning for my presence here. The qualities that define my existence here to me are shame and embarrassment. Yet others have an alternative view. They see good moral character and integrity. As I told this man, that I'm fond of, I only wish I could see myself as others do. I am stuck in this monstrous rut related to what I did, instead of whom I am and who I've been my entire life. People know me, even the people I associate with in prison have come to know me for who I truly am. More importantly is that I too, know myself. To once again come to the realization that what I did in no way is the totality of my identity. I've had hammered into me by the love of my life; through my biggest shame, my greatest accomplishment was birthed. The greatest gift within me produced the love, care and compassion that I have for others. Through it all, I want the remainder of my life to be as it was in this dream, and that is for God to remove my hands from the steering wheel of life, and just be *still* and allow Him to have complete control.

The time approached for another birthday to be spent in prison. This particular one seemed to be filled with more anguish than ones of the past, for I long to spend it with my love. What was even more agitating was learning that I wouldn't be able to talk with her on my birthday because she and her team were planning to visit a historical site in Egypt that day. It's joyous to my heart that she's fortunate enough to experience such chronicles of Biblical history. However, this day, though I would never tell her, selfishly, I wanted and needed her just for myself. This day; I needed her more. If even long enough just to hear that soft sweet voice say to me, *"Happy birthday baby!"*

When I talked with her several days prior to her departure, and although she knows me the way that she does, silently and secretly, I tried to conceal the hurt I felt so deep. Her voice told me that she could sense and feel all that was being withheld. That's the amazing thing about her and me, we know each other so profoundly and intensely at levels that truly have no depth. Even through all the miles that now disjoin us, she feels me. Our love and concern for the other will never be compromised, and the reason I know that is because she felt my suffering.

I tried to call her on Thursday, knowing we only had one other day to talk before my birthday, but I couldn't reach her. Instinctively, I became concerned because my attempts to reach her all day were futile. The fact that she is in a foreign country elevates my anxiety when I don't hear her voice each day. She and I have a pact. When I can't reach her for whatever reason, we both contact my mother as our go between. Again, this is our care and concern for each other, and it's something I've never had or experienced in my lifetime of relationships. When I called and spoke with my mother, I was told that the Internet service was down in Egypt. I felt so dejected, for I wanted her so much. Only she can cure this melancholy. Friday would be my early birthday present; that present being the sound of her voice.

Because she heard the heaviness in my voice, she spoke tenderly with me. I too could sense that she'd give anything to be with me at this moment. She'd give anything to be able to hold me and take away the sorrow I held within. Oddly, we didn't talk for long as her final words to me were, *"You know I would do anything for you."* Tears filled the cavity of my soul as I possessed the tenderness of her sensitivity. Little did I know how true these words would be.

The following morning, while in the shower, the pod C.O. called me for a visit earlier than usual. My mind raced with exuberance as I thought maybe my children had come to surprise me for my birthday. Little did I know that the exuberance I felt was for another reason. I thought I was walking on clouds in the midst of a daydream when I walked into the visiting room, for there she sat, the love of my life, appearing before me as an angel. She came all the way from Egypt for the sole purpose to be with me on my birthday. I whispered in her ear as we embraced, *"Baby what are you doing here?"* With the softest and sweetest voice I've ever heard, she replied, *"Happy birthday baby!"* Holding hands as we sat down, all I could mobilize in my mind was *"this woman is incredible!"* For several moments I could only sit and wonder in awe by the fact that only hours ago I thought I was talking with her from Egypt. And now I'm looking into her warm dove like eyes. Being overcome with emotions, I couldn't subdue the tears from streaming down my face. With a loving and gentle touch, she wiped my cheeks as the scent of her hands roused the core of my soul. *Oh* how I love this woman! After being stilled of my astonishment, and through my smiles and tears, I was finally able to gather my emotions enough to converse with her. Her smile lit the room as she explained to me that she and my mother had secretly been planning this for over a month. She explained to me that the day I couldn't reach her, she literally was on a plane from Cairo, Egypt destined for the United States; destined to get to me. During the time I talked with her just a day ago, she was actually in a hotel just miles away from C.R.C. She told about how she felt in some way that she was betraying me, and it was hard to keep this from me because we keep nothing from each other. Because she could hear and feel the hurt within me, she said she wanted so badly to tell me, *"I'm coming baby. Please feel me."*

Her unit's secretary in Egypt is someone who has become her close friend, and I learned that she is the one who helped to orchestrate her visit. She said that several times she had to call my mother and a close friend to calm her and keep her from letting the secret out. Oh how I loved her for this. If it's even possible, I love her more now than ever before. Once again, the world as I knew it became wondrous, as I looked into her warm eyes and held her soft tender hands. This day felt like the very first time we saw each other in over thirty years. It felt just as it did on 9 February, 2008.

We spent a beautiful weekend together, sharing and basking in the glow of each other's love. She solidifies every desire I've ever held within me. To think of her traveling this number of miles to be here for me, it left no wonder to the depth of love she has for me. She leaves only wonderment to her statement, *"You know, I'll do anything for you."*

At the end of our glorious weekend, she no sooner left my arms and I missed her. Never before in my life have I experienced anything like what she did for me this day. Never before have I known anyone like her. To me, she's the most *amazing* creature God has ever created; and I simply love her with everything within me.

Early one Saturday morning I had a conversation with a C.O. working the pod who happens to be a Christian. This is the same officer that I've had several conversations with concerning spiritual issues and the Bible. He called me over to the podium, and we began talking about faith and having strength in God. I explained that for the past few days I've really been going through a season of tiredness. It's not been a physical weakness, but rather one of being both emotionally and mentally exhausted. Quite simply, it's the old adage of being *"sick and tired, of being sick and tired!"* He tried to lift my spirits by telling me about how people around this institution view me as being or possessing something different than other inmates. He said, *"People have looked at you from a distance and said that you are a very humble and meek person, even if your stature doesn't show it."* He then shared with me intimate details concerning his life's past. I thought it was very unique what he shared with me because it paralleled my own life. He recalled the time that he was once working in the gym, and he called for me at the pod. It was a very cold winter evening, and at the time my love had just left for Egypt, and the last thing I wanted was conversation. Especially when I had to walk across the institution grounds in the cold to have it! Though in retrospect, this was a dialog, at that time, which I so badly needed. He reminded me about how he brought a Christian CD from home that day, for the sole purpose of listening to one particular song which was heartwarming to his spirit. It was upon hearing it that he felt a nudge from his spirit to call me over to the gym. He said, *"Do you remember that day? Remember you had a look on your face like I must be crazy to call you out in this cold?"* We both laughed as he continued, *"Remember me telling you not to be afraid in regard to your new found relationship with your first love, and me leaving you alone in the rec office, telling you to just listen to the words of that song?"* He rolled his chair closer to me and said, *"I remember coming back into the office, and tears were streaming down your face. I left home thinking that song was for me, but it was for you. I don't know where your heart was that day, but it was heavy. And God knew you needed to hear the words to that song."*

Just as it was that day, I was in need of this oral exchange. Of late I've been aching, longing, and churning so much within my soul to be with her that it has literally drained every ounce of emotion I possess. This is the expression of my tiredness. In the midst of our conversation, I was reminded of a verse of scripture in Hebrews that describes how Christ is touched with the feeling of our infirmities. With this C.O., once again being used as the vessel, God was making it known to me that He is aware of my hurt. I heard a profound statement once from a pastor I'd seen on television; *"When you hurt like you've never hurt before; you know you're almost there!"*

Through this time of hurt, affliction, and vexing in my soul, I'm doing all that I can to hold on just a little while longer. For I'm almost there.

⊰⬥⊱

As the next few months leisurely drifted away, the time came for my love to return from Egypt. Through countless hours of the days, weeks, and months that she's been away, I've grown to love and yearn for her to depths so unimaginable. During her absence, an unceasing and everlasting hunger for her has dominated me. One that only her presence can fulfill. *Oh,* how I've missed her!

Upon her return, she came to visit me. The instant that I beheld her beautiful face, I fell in love all over again. She enthralls me! With each visit, I become all encompassed and enchanted by the very sight and touch of her. We become more familiar with one another with each passing moment and opportunity that we're allotted to spend with each other. At one particular point, during a visit on Valentine's Day, we delved into a moment of intimacy that only the two of us and the Creator of the Universe could even begin to fathom. Never before have I felt such power and intensity as I felt at that fleeting moment while gazing into her eyes. It was as though on impulse our bodies communicated on a level I never thought could be attained. *AAh!* This woman is *so* in me! Never before have I known *such* profound passion and desire that is all captured in one enduring moment. I later received a Valentine's Day card from her that emphasized our belonging.

To My Love on Valentine's Day

One look at you is all it takes for me to fall in love all over again. Something in your smile makes me feel things I've never felt before. It's as if I'm discovering you, feeling love for the first time. One kiss from you is all it takes to remind me how special you are to me, how right we are for each other. One touch from you is all it takes to make me forget the rest of the world. Troubles and cares seem to vanish when we hold each other close. One night with you (soon), and I feel indescribably happy, as though I've been given one of the most precious gifts life has to offer – to love and be loved by you. Being with you, looking into your eyes, holding your hand, touching your cheek, is all it takes to convince me that Love was made just for us. "Happy Valentine's Day."

Within the card she wrote:

"You are the heart that beats inside of me. You are my home, my calm, my......I have always been yours."

Little does she know that from so long ago, I too, have always been hers.

<hr>

The time is vastly approaching for me to file for early release through the court system. With each passing day, I become more disquieted with the prospect of going home. It's been a long hard road to tread, yet, by the grace of God; I've pranced through every obstacle set before me. I'm tired. I'm so – so tired! It's like the old adage, *"I'm sick and tired, of being sick and tired!"* Over the past few days, I've noticed myself becoming more agitated and frustrated with my surroundings, and my spirit churns for deliverance. My endeavor to be released has become even more pronounced with thoughts about being with my love. Since she has come back into my life, she has brought a whole new perspective, meaning, and understanding to the word *freedom!* I so desperately long to be with her! She and I have come to know each other on so many levels, spiritually, emotionally, and mentally. The only level we've not yet obtained is the physical knowledge of one another. Every part of me craves to begin a life with her in this aspect. I deeply yearn to dwell in her presence.

I've been told that the number eight is symbolic for new beginnings. This being my eighth year of incarceration, I pray for this meaning to come to fruition and fulfillment in my life. Isaiah 43:18, 19 reads:

> *Remember ye not the former things, neither consider the things of old. Behold, I will do a new thing; now it shall spring forth; shall ye not know it? I will even make a way in the wilderness, and rivers in the desert.*

I'm reminded of a letter I once received from a family friend when she wrote, *"The second part of your life will be greater than the first. The best in your life is yet to come."* I pray that my filing of this paperwork is the dawning of new beginnings for my life. I pray also that the coming together with my love depicts what's yet to come. For *she*, my love, next to God and my children, is truly the best thing to ever have happened to me.

There came a period of time when a deep, somber impression of loneliness overtook me and held me captive for several days. I was more dreary, sad, and discontent than I ever recall feeling during my entire time of incarceration. Suddenly, I found it hard to exert any energy and just to make it through each passing day became excruciating. With intense desire, I could hear myself silently screaming for help, although there was no one to hear me. Though I eagerly sought for it through weeping, I found no solace. There was no one to catch my tears. Even more; it seemed that no one could truly understand. Ultimately, my mind and body increased in weariness, and I felt as though I was on a downward spiral with a direct course to depression.

One Tuesday morning during this dismal period, I spoke with the teacher at the school for whom I have great admiration. I told him about the infectious thoughts and feelings that have been afflicting my mind. I truly enjoy conversing with this man, and once more, just like previous talks with him, I withstood tears that I felt forming in my eyes. At one point, he gazed at me attentively and said, *"Luke you look pensive."* I replied, *"Sometimes I just think about things way too much! I seem to just always be in deep thought about something."* He then confirmed that which I had already felt as he told me that from all that I had shared with, he felt as though I was lonely. Simply, I replied, *"Yes I am."* We continued to talk briefly as the students began to arrive for class. I left his presence with a slight sense of vitality because I felt comfortable enough to open up and share my inner most emotions with him. At the end of the day, as he left for an appointment, I walked the institution grounds with him toward the front gate. Gently, he patted my shoulder, and caringly told me that he would say a prayer for me tonight. I'm so grateful and thankful for the person he is in spite of our circumstances.

Later that afternoon, when I ventured back to the pod, I had received a card from my oldest daughter. With each word as I read it, tears whelped in my eyes. Unbeknownst to her, the timing of this card was impeccable. It read:

> *The loving gifts you've given me as a father have shaped my life and made me the person I am...Your strong sense of values, of fairness, of right and wrong, are all a part of me. It makes me happy and proud to know that the qualities in you I love and admire so much are also a part of me. You are always with me, Dad...in my thoughts, in my heart, in the very fabric of my life. You are always with me.*

Then, in her words my daughter wrote:

> *"There is never a day that I don't think about you. You are with me in so many ways. I love you more than you will ever know!"*

Instantly, my spirit was revived and rejuvenated, as these words encased my heart entirely. As a father, I believe there is no greater joy than to be highly regarded by your child, and to for them to feel that all that is good within them she credits to you. As tears cascading down my face I found myself reading this card over and over again until I could rehearse the words in my mind. Throughout the stint of my lifetime, to include this time of incarceration; as a father, this was my proudest moment!

⋙•◆•⋘

One Sunday evening after a beautiful weekend visiting with the love of my life, I unexpectedly found me engrossed in conversation with another inmate regarding my love and me. He asked me a very intriguing question. *"Luke, do you ever look back and wonder as to why you're still here? Just think of the many times you've thought, or even felt that you were on the verge of being released. The clemency hearing, and of recent, the judicial release you filed – yet, God still has you here. Do you ever think that it could be due to God establishing something in you that you've never before had in your life – which is a foundation and stability with Him?* He continued; *"With all I know as to what you've shared regarding your relationship, it sounds as though neither you nor your new love have ever had a firm foundation built upon God. I believe that's why you're still incarcerated Luke; that God is taking this time to build within the both of you that which you've always lacked in your lives. Him!"* He paused, and in a brief moment of silence I sighed deeply. I breathed in the absorption of his words when suddenly without warning he continued. *"In you Luke she saw the good in what society deems and sees as a piece of brokenness. I bet from the first time that she ever wrote to you, and thereby, her judging your response back to her, she knew then at that very moment that she had found what she had been searching for all of her life. She found just as you did; the love of her life!"*

In listening to the words of this man, I could but only think in comparison to a passage of scripture in 2 Samuel 16:23, as it read, *"The council which this man gave was as if he had inquired at the oracle of God."* His observation caused me to reflect back to a statement that she once made to me after the renewal & rebirth of our undying love for one another. In her describing the feelings she's always had for me since childhood, she said to me; *"Where you are doesn't matter- but who you are means everything!"*

167

Later this same evening, I sat in the confines of my cell meditating intensely – my thoughts deeply immersed with our conversation. Forthwith, the spirit in me led me to Psalm 26: 2, 7;

> *Examine me, O Lord, and prove me; try my reins and my heart. That I may proclaim with the voice of thanksgiving, and tell of All Your wondrous works.*

To think that God has taken what seemingly appears to be the brokenness of my life, and through it has birthed His goodness in me. He's tried the reins and heart of this broken vessel, and fulfilled me with the beauty of His wonder. God has fulfilled a birth of foundation and stability both in Him, and with her; both are entities of which I have never before known in my life. Both of which I never again want to be without.

MYSTICAL HEARTBREAK

My soul deeply churned with anticipation upon waiting for a response in the filing of my judicial release paperwork. The spirit within me sought for relief as I so desperately yeaned to be home. Nevertheless, as the Christmas holiday vastly approached, so the prospect of being home became an immersing light, and my hopes began to diminish.

Frustration began to erupt within me with each failed attempt I made contact my attorney. Then, it came upon a day after distressing through the agony of waiting, that unexpectedly I was informed by the pod Sargent that I had legal mail to sign for. In my attempt to place my signature, the pen he *so respectfully* laid on the counter for me rattled between my fingers. Instantly, I became disheartened as I observed the words on the return address; *Montgomery County Common Pleas Court*. I raised my head for a brief moment from my eyes being fixated on this envelope enough to observe another inmate I had befriended intensely watching me – he too knowing that I was waiting upon a response from the court. As I traipsed the stairs to my cell, I grasped the envelope with such a feeling of uncertainty of its contents. This other inmate was in tow. Upon entering the confines of my cell, we stood facing one another in silence. Slowly, methodically, as my hands shuttered, I peeled open the envelope. Tears whelped in my eyes as I could but only glare at

the words: ***After reviewing the original pre-sentence investigation,
the defendant's request for Judicial Release is overruled – with
prejudice.***

With all I've overcome and conquered within myself after eight
years of incarceration, still, I'm being judged not based on who I am, but
rather by my past. I was denied without even being given a chance. And
just like that, it was over. It was made that I would never be able to file
again, the same opportunity that others are afforded. My friend stood
in astonishment as I read the words aloud. Watching the tears stream
down my face, he patted my shoulder and said, *"I'm so sorry Luke."* He
told me that he would give me some time to myself. And with that, he
turned and left me standing in my cell the same way my soul felt. Alone!

There's a passage in the book of Revelation where John describes
concerning Jesus that he, *"Fell at His feet as dead."* With tears racing
down my face like a watercourse, there in my cell on the cold concrete
floor; I laid prostate like a dead man before the Lord. *Oh!* How I cried!
It seemed as though this hurt far surpassed that of my first arrival here.
I wept vehemently!

In despair, as soon as count was clear, I placed an agonizing call to
my love. Immediately, hearing the desperation and intensity in my voice
she asked, *"Baby what's wrong?"* Weeping bitterly, I was able to muster,
"They turned me down!" She became frantic; for this was a side of me
she hadn't yet been exposed to. It was a side that I myself was unsure
of. Painstakingly, yet lovingly, she began to console me. As a stream
of emotions bolted through me, gently, she read the 23rd Psalm to me,
along with other comfortable passages of scripture. The gentleness of
her voice soothed me, and alleviated the torment within my heart. I
needed her; my best friend, and she was there for me. I wept bitterly
with her over the phone, uncaring of the possibility of being watched
by other inmates. *Oh, how I hurt!* After lying in my bunk silently crying
all through the night, I woke the next day and placed a call to my
attorney. Bluntly and plainly he told me that I was simply being judged
because of me being a State Trooper. He informed me that the judge
and prosecutor could not seem to get past that fact. Even with all I've
accomplished and come through after being incarcerated for 8 ½ years

I'm still being ridiculed and looked upon for my past occupation. A State Trooper was what I was, it's not who I am. In the eyes of the court, that's all I ever will be remembered as. It seems that the same career passion of my life will also be that which will torment me.

For the next few days, tears exuded from my eyes and my strength was depleted. Overridden with emotions, I agonized over a phone call I knew had to be made. It was time once again to be that little boy calling on his mother for help to ease a pain. And once again, she was there. As the salty taste of tears cascaded down my cheeks and onto my quivering lips, I cried to her. *"Momma, I just don't understand! I just don't understand!"* Then, as only a loving mother could, in her own unique way, with solace she said; *"I know you don't understand Luke. I know. None of us do. We don't know what God is doing, but we have to trust Him. Just hold on and don't give up. We have to trust Him."* Like as a child who just received a bandage for a scar, her words healed me. Silently, I muttered, *"Ok Mom."*

A week or so removed from my anguish, I was contacted by a dear cousin who expressed her tenderhearted and unfeigned sympathy. She told me that she knows that I must feel defeated and depleted, but through it all we're in this together! Through my entire stint of incarceration I've always told myself that if ever I were to marry again, I'd be honored to have her at my side. Subsequently, I learned that this decision from the court reached to depths unbeknownst to me. I was told that my daughter and my brother-in-law all shed tears of their own. Upon a card I received from my love's mother I learned that others outside of my family were also touched by my misfortune. The card read:

> *On the journey of life, every tomorrow is a path waiting to be walked. Seek out what makes you happy. Keep moving in the direction of your dreams. If the past weighs you down, leave behind those things that can't be changed... Leave behind each "should have" and "If only." Travel lightly and carry only what you need – hope, love, and belief in yourself. Every step, no matter how small, will*

> *take you somewhere until one day, you'll look back at how*
> *far you've come...and be amazed. Remember...you're not*
> *alone. Others are beside you, believing in you and looking*
> *forward to the day when life is much better for you.*

Not only was I take a back, but was also astonished with her benevolence! These words touched me, and I was extremely grateful.

As endless days dawned, my tears abated, and the agony subsided. Yet, still and all, the utility of both never fully left me. Their presence still remains.

One morning, when taking a brief interlude from class, I was approached by an inmate who works in the institution library. He addressed me placidly and said, *"Luke, I want to talk to you about something."* I looked a little puzzled as in a mutter he continued, *"I've been going through some personal things in my life, and I don't know how to deal with it. I heard something about you, and I've wanted to come and talk with you but I didn't know how to approach you."* Instantly, I understood his subdued undertone, and I stated, *"You're talking about what I did with the Parole Board during my clemency hearing."* He seemed to sink within himself with astonishment to my directness, and modestly he replied, *"Yes. I really need to know how you found that inner strength to be able to do what you did."* I instantly alleviated his passivity by telling him to feel free to come and talk with me whenever he's ready.

Taken aback, I traipsed back down the hallway to my classroom. My thoughts were fixed on how he learned about the acts of my clemency hearing. I thought both of how and why it was even being discussed; how after the time that has since passed, the furtherance of that decisive day of my life unbeknown to me is still being recalled by others. However puzzled, for some peculiar reason, I couldn't help but smile, which truly mystified me. So, later this same evening in the pod, this same inmate began to confer with me about *"ghosts of his past."* He confided in me of the possibility of criminal charges pending from a neighboring state. He told me that though being previously incarcerated, this stint of incarceration has bought about a change in him. He stated that he's been evaluating his life, and has

172

since given his life over to the Lord. That, he stated, is what led him to me. He stood, arms crossed over his chest, and told me how after hearing of my confession before the Parole Board members during my clemency hearing, compelled him to own up to his transgressions and wrong doings which now plagues him. As if interpreting the thoughts in my mind, undaunted, he uttered, *"Luke I won't say who, but just being honest with you; someone made the comment that 'Luke made it hard for anyone who goes before the Parole Board, they're going to think we're all lying!"* Usually, I wouldn't entertain any further exchange of conversation or dialog after being told, *"I won't say who, but somebody said!"* Howbeit, I made an exception this time. He went on to inquire of me; *"Luke, tell me please; how did you find the inner strength to be able to do what you did?"* Without ambiguity or hesitation, I simply stated, *"God. It truly had nothing to do with me, because I would not, and could not have done it on my own. It had everything to do with Christ in me. He enabled me to correct the wrong in my heart, and to make it right. It was doing as you openly self-admitted; giving my life to the Lord, and allowing Him to lead and guide me. It was His voice which spoke through me that day, saying 'No' when being asked if this was an accident. I believe it's that same voice which speaks to you now, telling you the right thing to do. It's merely a matter now of you doing it."* With that, tears forming his eyes, he reached forth his hand and shook mine saying, *"Thank you. I knew that it was meant for me to talk to you. I know now what I have to do."*

As he walked away, that mystified smile reappeared, and I could only ponder on God's goodness. Once again, it made me recount that time that I was told by a C.O. that I truly admire that he's used my actions of that day as a testament with parishioners as to true Christian conduct. However, I thought of how a moment of being freed spiritually, yet left bound physically for myself bought forth such freedom to another. It left me to reflect on a verse of scripture. Romans 8: 18 reads:

> *For I reckon that the suffering of this present time are not worthy to be compared with the glory which shall be revealed in us.*

This signifies the reason of my mystical smile.

———⟫◆⟪———

In reflecting back to the time period after my incident occurred, and prior to me being charged with felonious assault, it's become apparent that God is bringing into fruition a statement once made to me by one of my sisters. She told me that she knew why I was going through, and facing all that I was. Simply put, she said, *"Jail ministry!"* I remember at the time having the same notion, albeit, never did the notion conclude in me taking the route of incarceration; being in the very midst of those to whom I would be ministering to. However, I'm reminded of a phrase my mother has made on occasion during visits with me; *"If you want to make God laugh, just make plans on your own."*

Of late, since first being approached by the inmate regarding my actions during my clemency hearing, I've found myself being approached more often for counsel, and ministering the Word of God to more and more guys, both staff and inmate. For a time period, with the guidance of the Holy Spirit, I've been sharing and teaching an inmate of devout Muslim faith about true salvation found only in Jesus Christ. As he spoke boldly regarding his beliefs, and as to not offend, I construed the *true* Word of God to him. As a passage reads in Acts 18:26 regarding *"I took him and expounded upon him the way of God more accurately."*

There also came a day that I spent an evening ministering in the cell of two other inmates. Suddenly, one of whom was of Guatemalan decent, tenderly rested his head back against the wall and began to cry. Instantly, I was moved with compassion, and I told him to take his time as he sobbed and struggled to utter words through a weighty English dialect. Through an abundance of tears he said, *"I always try to learn from others, but I no understand! I hear God speak to me as you talk to me Luke. You have a gift. Thank you Luke, thank you. You have a gift. God is good, I hear Him!"* His body convulsed as he attempted to catch his breath. Through tears, he again said with a smile, *"You teach me good Luke. Thank you!"*

Count time loomed, and with that, I withdrew to my cell. I crawled onto my bunk and simply muttered *"Thank you Jesus!"* Had it not been for the presence of my cellmate, I would have collapsed in tears of my own. The lyrics to a song titled, *"I give myself away so you can use me,"* lingered in my head as it disintegrated onto my pillow; silently, I succumbed, and thanked Him for counting me worthy to be used for His glory.

⟫◆⟪

I've been absent from, and missed out on many happenings during my stint of incarceration. Albeit of late, two monumental milestones have unequivocally melted the core of my heart. Those both being of me coming to the knowledge of my oldest daughter's engagement of marriage, and learning of the birth of my first grandchild with my younger daughter. As a father, with the prospect of both delights, instantaneously becoming a father-in-law and a grandpa, I beam with pride!

I was immersed with a stream of immense affection and appreciation when it came upon a day that I received a letter from my now future son-in-law. In it, he requested my permission to have my daughter's hand in marriage. Furthermore, learning also that he and my daughter are unwavering in electing not to have the marriage ceremony until I'm home; both wanting me to walk my baby down the aisle. To be thought of, and regarded in such esteem, not only by my daughter but her fiancé' as well; in that, I'm humbled beyond words.

Subsequently, one of the most joyous days and moments of my life came when placing a phone call to my love and my mother and hearing from both, *"Hi papaw, and congratulations!"* Never before have I experienced or felt such an exuberance of joy! To fathom; my little baby having a baby of her own. Soon after the phone receiver departed from my hand, I proceeded to my cell and could feel the implosion of tears forming from the depths of my heart. I quickly nabbed a hand full of starlight mints, and proceeded to pass them around to various choice inmates, saying with exuberance to each, *"I'm a grandpa!"* The only event that comes in comparison to this bliss was when three years ago, my first love came back into my life. Though two separate entities of events, nonetheless, both were astounding sources of meaning for new beginnings in my life. I call to mind two Biblical scriptures; separate, yet equal with regard to these two occasions. Revelation 2: 4, 6;

> *Nevertheless I have this against you, that you have left your first love. Remember therefore from where you have fallen.*

And also Joel 2: 25, 26;

> *So I will restore to you the years that the locust hath eaten, the cankerworm, and the caterpillar, and the palmerworm; And ye shall eat in plenty, and be satisfied, and praise the name of the Lord your God, that hath dealt wondrously with you.*

Just as God brought me back full circle to where I had fallen to my first love, through the wonderful gift of birth of my grandchild, He's also restored back to me all the years I've lost with my loving children. Though I have enough knowledge to know that I can never recover the years lost, however, with God, I believe the restoration with both entities is going to be far greater than what I could ever imagine. With God's grace, I believe the best is yet to come. With the birth of these two new beginnings in my life, in this, I'm satisfied. I'm filled. For He, has dealt wondrously with me.

⟖⬥⟗

With the passing of each evening, I find myself to be more and more involved in the sharing, teaching and ministering of the Word of God with the inmate from Guatemalan decent. Never before have I met a man who bears such a hunger and thirst for knowledge and understanding of God and His ways. One night, I opened my heart to him, and shared with him my story. Once more, as at other times he silently, yet openly, cried in my presence. It seems as though with each encounter that we have together, he becomes overridden with emotion. On one particular evening, as we stood on the top range of the pod, I shared with him the story of King David, and spoke to him about the grace of God. Suddenly, he appeared to be fighting back tears and I noticed his eyes become extremely red. Broken, he said to me, *"Now I understand Luke. God is so good, I understand His grace. I don't tell anyone this, ever, but I feel so comfortable with you. I commit adultery long ago. I was married in Guatemala, and then I left and come here to United States. You understand, yes? I come here and get married, and have three children. As you talk to me about David, and the penalty of sin, God show me, and I understand that my being here is good! It's good because I have to pay the penalty for what I done. The Bible say that you reap what you sow right? So I reap by being here. Yes, God is good. I now understand! I Love this Luke. Please continue to teach me. God talk to me through you!"* Just as with other times, I went to my cell and shed tears of my own. Each time spent with this man ends with a whisper; *"Thank you Jesus!"* In my ministering with him I again reflect of the day standing before the parole board. As each time, in broken dialect, this man's voice resonates in my ear; *"I know why you here Luke. God have you here for me. To-to help me! Thank you Luke!"*

<hr />

I once read an entry from a daily devotional entitled *"Prisoner to Prisoner"* which was shown to me by another inmate. In reading it, it was as though looking into a mirror of words which was the memoir of my life. It read:

"Dying To Live"

The hardest thing that I have ever done was confessing my crime to my family and friends. I was afraid of prison, but mostly I was afraid of letting their image of me die. It was a false image, a lie, and it needed to die. I needed to confess my crimes, to come clean before my family before I could ever be healed and restored. I did not want to come to prison; I did not want to be punished, but it was a right and necessary thing. By confessing my crimes I was able to stop pretending to be a good man and begin to actually be a good man. Living in sin is a hard burden to bear; it feels easier to lie. But every lie must die. Confessing our sins, repenting of them, and turning to God are the only ways that we find healing. This is a death, but this death is not the end; it is only the beginning of something new and wonderful.

What God placed on my heart to do that day made no sense to so many; yet, it impacted the lives of others.

⊰◈⊱

A day removed from talking with the Guatemalan inmate, I received a letter from a high school classmate, who happens to attend church with my daughter. In my daughter speaking so proudly of her dad, he asked my permission to share my story with individuals he counsels with substance abuse through their church. He told me that my story is so inspirational, and will touch so many. Again, I marvel at the works of God. So in this, I realize that I had to die; in order for others to live.

LAST DAYS

As another Father's Day approaches, my heart melts with the realization of this being my last one spent within the confines of these prison walls. *Ah!* It's as though I can literally taste the dew of freedom on my heart, like as sweet drops of honeycomb to my lips.

As I glare out of my cell window to an opened field just adjacent to the wire fence surrounding the prison compound, I can't help but wonder if next year at this time will the scent of freedom on the other side of the fence bear the same fragrance of aroma as that I so long for. For many waking days and sleepless nights; I wonder.

Two days prior to the arrival of Father's Day, I received cards from my loving children. I gleamed with joy as I read a card from my newly born grandchild – myself proclaimed little man. Along with an outlined sketch of his tiny little hand, the words, *"To Paw Paw-can't wait to meet you"* simply warmed my heart. I too, cannot wait to meet him for the very first time. Albeit, the card that affected me the most was one sent by my oldest daughter. This card was as if it had been hand written from within her heart; for it spoke directly to the situation at hand. It read:

> *Dad,*
>
> *I'll never know everything you've been through or all the feelings you carry quietly in your heart…I just know that somehow all your rich experience has made you the wise and loving man you are – someone who's taught me that time is precious and laughter is sweet, that I'm brave and smart,*

and that no one knows me better than I know myself…
So much of the woman I've become has been influenced by
you. And as you celebrate today, I'm celebrating too, and
honoring you – my very first hero, my wonderful dad.

In her own words she wrote: *"I love you more than you will ever know.*
You are and will always be my number 1 guy."

I could but only marvel both with the wording of the card itself, and those of her own. I've grown to understand through experience of daily rigor with other inmates that prison life can have such a negative impact on families. Just as I've always felt and exclaimed, those in your life who truly love you, and are toiling through this prison experience with you, in a sense, they too are incarcerated. Albeit, not physically, but in all other ways plausible they themselves are imprisoned. They are what I've once entitled, *"The other side of the sentence!"* To know that my daughter feels that she is who she is, and that I've become who I am now through and because of this, astounds the realm of my thoughts. She may not know everything that I've been through, or the quiet feelings I hold within my heart; but to know that she honors me, and looks upon me as her very first hero, and number one guy; for me, in that, she knows enough. Although my daughter may not understand the burdens I carry, just as her card read, she does understand one point which I feel to be most important. She understands me. As a dad, be it on Father's Day or any other, that's a treasure within itself.

Lastly, the weekend was culminated with a visit from my love. Um… gazing into her warm dove eyes, and feeling the soft touch of her gentle hands left lasting impressions of Father's Days to come. I read a card from her, or as she and I have titled our mail correspondence; *"My kiss!"* It read:

You are the strong tree that lifts me gently toward the sun,
holds me firmly in the storm, sends roots down – down,
deeper and deeper, grounding me, nurturing me with your
love. You give me everything I need and could ever want.
I Love you baby.

In reading *my kiss,* a passage of scripture was placed on my heart. Jeremiah 8:18.

> *When I would comfort myself against sorrow, my heart is faint in me.*

It was the roots of the tree of my heart that needed nurture and strength as I held her firmly in my arms that Sunday afternoon upon the end of visiting. Even with it being my last Father's Day incarcerated, my heart fainted within me as she departed. For on this day she gave me everything that I needed.

———◆———

It came upon a day that rumors were running rampart around the institution that all cadre inmates were being transferred to other institutions. However, for me, I viewed them as what I've entitled *"Inmate.com!"* Albeit, just as a passage in Daniel 7:28 reads;

> *As for me, my cogitations much troubled me, and my Countenance changed in me: but I kept the matter in my heart.*

One of my greatest fears while being incarcerated has been that of one day being transferred to another prison. So though my mind may have discarded it, my heart captured every thought.

Then one afternoon while leaving the education building from work, I noticed several white shirted institution officers entering the pod from afar off. Upon entering the pod, there stood the institutions' warden, arrayed by a flank of officers, to include the institution major. The upper and lower tier of the pod was flanked with all of the cadre inmates. It was when the warden began to speak that my greatest fear came into fruition. She stated plainly of CRC going through some changes that will directly affect all of the cadre inmates. We learned the camp was being converted into a close security facility, and due to that, we all would be transferred to other institutions throughout the state. Instantly, my heart sunk to my stomach and breathing became a task I found hard to achieve! After a barrage of questions, it seemed in an instant, it was over. The warden left the pod, flanked by her entourage. For the first time of incarceration I experienced something most uncomfortable, yet extraordinary; an aura of stilled *"hush"* across the pod. I saw within the many faces the same thing I felt in my heart, that being that no one wanted to leave. For once, in solidarity, all cadre inmates stood on common ground.

In the several weeks to come, several meetings were held concerning myself as to where I should be transferred to. I was told by the unit manager that due to my background I was best suited for an institution called Franklyn Pre-Release. I learned that this institution formerly housed low security female inmates, but now houses low security males. He said to me directly that this is the best place for me – a gift in my lap. I, however, knew this not to be Christmas, and he certainly was not Santa Claus! Albeit, his thoughts concerning me was confirmed by several other staff members of whom I had more trust in, reiterating his same sentiments. I conferred regularly with my family, my love and several institution staff members, all of which vehemently tried to convince me that if I had to leave CRC, this institution seemed to be the next best place to be. So, in the midst of my anguish, and after many discussions it was settled. Within the next few weeks I was to be transferred to Franklyn Pre –Release Center.

A month or so removed from the time the warden first came to the pod and gave her all cadre exodus speech, it was thought on several occasions that my time for leaving CRC had come, only to be delayed time & time again. Though we both knew it to be inevitable, my cellmate and I never discussed the move. Over these past nine plus years, he and I had become very close, and very familiar with the other. Spending so much time in a 10 by 12 cell with another person can either break you, or bring respect to each other. We had that; respect, trust, and understanding that two men could ever achieve in un-natural conditions. In the whole stint of my incarceration, no other two inmates celled together as long as we had. No others even came close. We never argued, never fought, and never had one disagreement.

He had become a friend, a brother. Though our paths are soon to part, I will never forget him.

Strangely, one evening while walking the institution track, several guys who befriended me approached me with words of gender and handshakes. Some gave stern hugs and pats on the pack, telling me how I've impacted and touched their lives; how they valued and respected the way I did my time. I was captivated and taken aback by their words and gestures towards me. Oddly, it was as though they knew this to be the only opportunity to express these sentiments to me prior to me leaving. One inmate in particular, whom I had a spiritual bond with stood with tears whelping in eyes. From what I felt to be from the core of his soul, he said, *"Man Luke! I'm going to miss you dude! I'm so glad I got to know you, even in this place. You are a good dude. I learned a lot from you. You take good care."* It wasn't until the following morning that I realized what these other inmates had somehow already known. Unbeknownst to me, the steps around the institution track that night would be my last. At 6:00 am the following morning, I was awakened by the pod officer and told simply, *"Pack your things, you're riding out!"*

I suddenly found myself overcome with emotion as I fought back tears. With my cellmate already being gone to work, I looked out of my cell window as if for the last time. My bags were packed, yet, I was unprepared. Even after all these years of incarceration and coming to know the ends and outs of prison life, once more, I was frightened. As count time cleared, I was again approached by a herd of inmates expressing their goodbyes to me. I was overwhelmed! Albeit, departing from my cellie was by far the most gut wrenching! As I gathered my bags amongst hugs and gestures from so many, I heard a voice almost in a whisper say, *"Here he comes!"* It was then when I happened to look up and see my cellmate enter the pod. All seemed to fall silent, and a direct path was made from him to me. Instantly, I felt a gush of tears wail inside me; tears of which I could not contain. We met atop the stairs on the top tier, and with all watching, the inevitable happened. We fell into each other's arms and wept bitterly for all to see. No words were spoken...no words were needed. Our tears spoke for us. And with that, we turned and walked away. There was nothing left to say.

During a toilsome out-processing period, I was amazed of all the staff members who personally came to the out-processing area to give to me their sentiments. This was another rare occasion due to the affairs of difference that was embarked between staff and inmate. Yet, these staff members in their own way looked upon me as one once among their ranks, simply fell from grace. It touched me deeply.

As my ankles were being shackled, and a chain being placed around my waist connected to handcuffs on my wrists, I could but only think of the day I was first transported here. My ankles riddled with pain as the shackles pierced into my bone as I shuffled onto a large institution transportation bus. The only difference between this time and the last is nine plus years of incarcerated life. The shackle and chains are no less demeaning. They still hurt the bone as well as the soul. I still hurt!

With each mile traipsed, the bus was unforgiving as it shook and raddled furiously. I wasn't even afforded the opportunity to view the outside world due to the windows being obscured by cages. Sensing the proximity of our destination, exasperated, I gulped back tears. As the bus exited the interstate and seemingly directly onto the prison compound, silently I whispered in my heart, *"Lord, cover me with Your divine favor!"*

Upon being escorted into the institution I found the processing stage to be not as formidable as it was several years ago. After going through all that processing entails I was taken to my new assigned cell, thus beginning the tumultuous task of getting settled into a new routine; or as the prison dialect terms as *"Get into my bit!"* Although, in observing my surroundings it became evident that I would miss CRC and all the people I had come to know for over nine years. The atmosphere was different in every way. For the first time since my transfer I was finally able to place a call to my love. In the frustration of not being able to talk with her for days, together, we wept in harmony. Upon hearing her voice a passage of tears exuded through the phone line. I uttered to her, *"I feel so lost!"* Struggling to surmount her emotions, with eloquence she told me, *"Hold on baby, God's got you!"* Tenderly, we consoled each other with the notion of it all being over in a few more months. With that, for the next few months I fought within myself to get into a routine. It was as though I struggled to find myself all over again.

⟐

In this time of my adjustment of change, I learned of an enduring reflection which captivated my mother's heart. During a phone conversation, she spoke of how amazing it felt knowing that my time of incarceration was finally reaching its summit. With the concerned voice of a mother she asked, *"Luke do you think the media will be there when you are released?"* At that moment, then too was my mind was taken aback. I thought of the many days endured during my trial when my face was a fixture for the local news stations. I then absorbed a sense of apprehension as my mother began to explain to me that her concern is based due to a day in the courtroom unbeknownst to me. She accounted, *"All during your trial, I was unable to go into the courtroom. I just couldn't bear it! Then when it came time for the verdict to be rendered, everybody felt that I should be in there. They coerced me by saying, 'what would it look like with his mother not being in the courtroom for the reading of the verdict?"* Instantly, I felt my emotions on the brink to unravel as she continued. *"The one thing through all of this that I have never been able to erase from my mind is how you looked at me when they put handcuffs on you. As they walked you out you turned and looked straight back at me. I've never told you this, but I'll never forget the look on your face. It haunts me to this day."* She then recounted the newspaper article detailing, *"The last thing he did was to look back at his mother."* A sudden quietness gushed across the phone as passion for my mother wrenched inside of me! I struggled to constrain the surge of moisture forming within my eyes as a watercourse. I felt it within her too! Without it being spoken, deep within our hearts we knew the sentiment of that day will forever be a plastered memory. There's a passage of scripture which comes to mind regarding this account. Job 3:1 reads;

After this opened Job his mouth, and cursed his day.

After this, I too abhor that fatal day of memory in breaking my mother's heart. I'd give anything to take that moment back.

⟫◆⟪

A last, after ten years of imprisonment, the time of my release is finally at hand. Just as the sun sets on each passing day, so sets my heart to the furtherance of home. A deep reflection of the past ten years clouds my thoughts as the sweet aroma of freedom looms in the air. In looking into the mirror of my soul I reflected on a message brought forth during a Sunday morning church service. The minister's sermon was titled, *"A good man in a bad situation."* She said, *"You need to see yourself as God sees you. You are a good man in a bad situation. You can be a good man, yet, still find yourself in a storm, just like Job. Just as his friends did him, people will try and judge you for your past. But know that what you did doesn't describe who you are! God's got you!"* She continued, *"You've dealt with pain, with struggle, and with being sick and tired of being sick and tired! It's been meant for you, to know who you are! All the pain, the loss of loved ones, the storms of life; God has kept you, and been in the midst of you. This thing has been spiritual!"* Throughout the duration of her message I simply cried! The same stream of tears which flowed down my face was the same which flowed within my heart. I thank God! Because of Him, I don't look like where I've came from, or what I've been through! The apostle Paul wrote in Philippians 3:13,

> *I count not myself to have apprehended: but this one Thing I do, forgetting those things which are behind, And reaching forth unto those things which are before.*

No longer will I live by my mistakes and ghosts of my past. Through it all, I can say with all sincerity, *"It was good for me that I was afflicted! For it has made me who I am!* Many may ask or even wonder, *"How did you do it? How did you make it through ten years of being in prison as a State Trooper?"* The answer for me is a simple one. **God kept me, every step of the way!**

⎯⎯⎯◆⎯⎯⎯

The morning has finally arrived! My day has at last come! I was told by one officer that I had a large gathering of family who had just arrived at the institution. Several guys arose early to see me off, which touched me deeply. As the corrections officer came to escort me, they all went to the small rec yard area and lined themselves along the fence which was just adjacent to the road leading away from the prison grounds to await my departure. The officer escorting me said that in all of his years of service as an officer; he has never seen anything like that.

As he opened that last door leading to the parking lot where my family was waiting, I could smell a distinct aroma that I've longed for; the air of freedom! As we turned the corner of a building, sheer adoration of joy erupted from the parking lot as my family laid eyes on me. A burst of emotion overcame me, and my knees wobbled with the realization of these being my last steps taken in confinement! As one officer stood at the gate, the escorting officer turned to me with his hand extended and said, *"Good luck to you man."* And with that, I was a free man!

I fell into my baby sister's arms and we wept bitterly! She held me tightly as with the fear of not wanting to lose me again. I then turned to my mother and other family members who were all sheading this time tears of joy! I was then approached by a corrections officer who was one I knew from CRC. He approached and told me that there was something he has wanted to do for a long time. He then extended his hand and firmly took mine, simultaneously pulling me into him. Looking me squarely in the eye he told me that I was a good guy, and that I was going to do well out there. Tears whelped in his eyes as he turned and walked away.

As we exited the institution grounds, so many inmates were aligned the circumference of the fence. They all waived and yelled as our entourage of vehicles passed by for the last time. Inside the lead car, I

187

wept vehemently so, leaving tears of memories behind. For now I can finally say as it reads in 2 Timothy 4:7,

I have fought a good fight, I have finished my course, I have kept the faith.